the Weekend Crafter®

Rubber Stamp Carving

the Weekend Crafter®

Rubber Stamp Carving

Techniques, Designs & Projects

LUANN UDELL

LARK
BOOKS

A Division of Sterling
Publishing Co., Inc.
New York

EDITOR:
JOANNE O'SULLIVAN

ART DIRECTOR & PRODUCTION:
CHRIS BRYANT

COVER DESIGN:
BARBARA ZARETSKY

PHOTOGRAPHY:
EVAN BRACKEN

ILLUSTRATIONS:
ORRIN LUNDGREN

PROJECT DESIGNER:
TERRY TAYLOR

EDITORIAL ASSISTANCE:
VERONIKA ALICE GUNTER
RAIN NEWCOMBE
NATHALIE MORNU
HEATHER SMITH

PRODUCTION ASSISTANCE:
HANNES CHAREN

DEDICATION

For my husband Jon, with love, awe, and respect, for his constant support and encouragement.

And for my children Robin and Doug—by dreaming good things for you, I learned to dream for myself again.

Library of Congress Cataloging-in-Publication Data
Available.

10 9 8 7 6 5 4 3 2 1

First Edition

Published by Lark Books, a division of
Sterling Publishing Co., Inc.
387 Park Avenue South, New York, N.Y. 10016

© 2002, Luann Udell

Distributed in Canada by Sterling Publishing,
c/o Canadian Manda Group, One Atlantic Ave., Suite 105
Toronto, Ontario, Canada M6K 3E7

Distributed in the U.K. by:
Guild of Master Craftsman Publications Ltd.
Castle Place, 166 High Street Lewes, East Sussex, England BN7 1XU
Tel: (+ 44) 1273 477374 Fax: (+ 44) 1273 478606
Email: pubs@thegmcgroup.com, Web: www.gmcpublications.com

Distributed in Australia by Capricorn Link (Australia) Pty Ltd.,
P.O. Box 704, Windsor, NSW 2756 Australia

The written instructions, photographs, designs, patterns, and projects in this volume are intended for the personal use of the reader and may be reproduced for that purpose only. Any other use, especially commercial use, is forbidden under law without written permission of the copyright holder.

Every effort has been made to ensure that all the information in this book is accurate. However, due to differing conditions, tools, and individual skills, the publisher cannot be responsible for any injuries, losses, and other damages that may result from the use of the information in this book.

If you have questions or comments about this book, please contact:
Lark Books
67 Broadway
Asheville, NC 28801
(828) 236-9730

Printed in China

ISBN 1-57990-300-2

CONTENTS

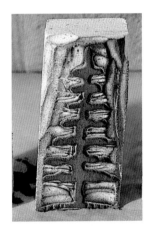

INTRODUCTION

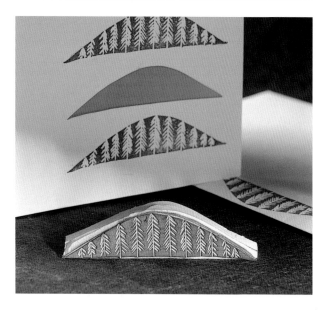

WELCOME TO THE WONDERFUL WORLD OF CARVING STAMPS!
Pull up your chair, grab a block of carving material and some tools, and ignore your clock. This book is your very own personal, stamp-carving workshop. Get ready to embark on a new artistic journey—one that is simple, accessible, fulfilling, and fun!

Whether you're an avid rubber stamper, a collage artist, a printmaker, or a curious beginning crafter, carving your own rubber stamps gives you the opportunity to learn new skills, use your imagination, and create images that are completely, uniquely your own.

If you've never thought of carving your own stamps before, now is the perfect time to start. Just a few decades ago, carving rubber stamps was known only to mail artists who carved tiny white vinyl erasers and exchanged their images with fellow artists through the post. Today this up-and-coming craft combines tools from linoleum block carving, techniques from rubber stamping and printmaking, and common office supply materials to create a versatile, accessible form of art that just about anyone can enjoy.

Why carve your own stamps when there are hundreds of stamp companies offering thousands of stamps for every conceivable area of interest?

Let's start with the purely practical reasons. Carving your own stamps is cheaper than buying commercially produced stamps. Rubber stamping can be quite an expensive hobby. You may find yourself paying a small fortune to get all the images you want. When you carve your own images, you need only invest in a few inexpensive materials and a little bit of time.

In addition, carving your own stamps is convenient. You can produce your own images when it seems impossible to find just the right one. Whatever project you're working on, your hand-carved stamp will give it an unmistakable charm and personal quality that you just can't get from a commercial stamp.

Nowadays, it's easier than ever to find the supplies and information you need. Mail-order companies, craft stores, and websites offer a variety of carving materials ranging from traditional white vinyl erasers to larger blocks in different colors, textures, and sizes. Stamping magazines and online carving communities offer information and suggestions to the new carver, making it simple to find tips and advice. In fact, there's a large, active carving community around the world.

Learning to carve stamps is quick and easy. A few introductory lessons send most new carvers happily on their way. Simple efforts can result in a beautifully rendered image, and basic designs can produce surprisingly sophisticated stamps. As a teacher, I often hear my adult students express doubts about their abilities before they start a class. Later, they often leave with work I feel is better than my own!

Practicality aside, carving your own stamps is appealing on a much more profound level. Envisioning an image to carve, choosing how you will treat it, editing its aspects, and then carving it with your own unique style move you to a level of creativity you may never have thought possible. The process of selecting, translating, and synthesizing each element is really the process of creating art.

You may start out thinking "I'm not an artist," "I can't draw," or "I'm not creative," but carving can bring out the artist in you in ways you may have never experienced before. You'll realize your individual way of seeing the world (through the images you choose) and your individual way of translating that vision (through your way of carving). You *are* the artist you've always dreamed of being!

DID I MENTION THAT IT'S EASY AND FUN?

The Getting Started section of this book reviews the materials and tools you'll need to start carving, and introduces basic techniques. You'll progress from making simple strokes to carving borders and creating positive and negative images. The Troubleshooting section will advise you on how to correct problems in your carving. Then you'll find 20 great stamps to carve for practice, as well as ideas for beautiful things to make with your stamps. Finally, the Gallery will introduce you to the range of work carvers are creating today—these images will inspire you!

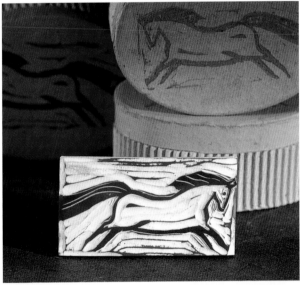

From the moment I saw my artist friend effortlessly carve a little dog bone stamp for me, I thought, "I want to do that, too!" She showed me how, right then and there. I thought it would be hard, but it wasn't. I thought it would take time to get good at it, but it didn't. I thought I would run out of ideas, but I haven't.

I wish I could sit down next to you and carve a little dog bone stamp for *you*, but I can't, so I wrote this book instead. Read a little, learn a little, try a little, and carve a lot!

GETTING STARTED:
MATERIALS, TOOLS & TECHNIQUES

A variety of custom-made and commercial carving materials

Work Space

All you really need to get started is a place to sit and work, good light, carving material, and a set of carving tools (see page 10). You can work on any flat, stable surface—a kitchen or dining room table, a folding table, or a desk (use a cutting mat to protect your work surface). You can also simply hold the carving block in one hand and carve with the other.

Work in a comfortable position. If you experience neck or hand strain, adjust your position. Keep a wastebasket handy and sweep your eraser crumbs into it when you're done. See Storing Your Images on pages 24–25 for ideas on how to store your stamps.

If you have wall space for it, keep a small bulletin board near you for ideas and inspiration. You can tack up inspirational quotes (solemn and funny), images you intend to carve, prints of your favorite carved images, snippets of fabric, exotic paper, or a brilliant fall leaf.

Carving Materials

Despite the fact that it's almost always described as rubber, most carving material is made of a soft vinyl eraser-like substance. It can be found in a variety of shapes, sizes, and degrees of thickness and density. It is usually cream-colored, but can be found in other colors, or even multicolored blocks, such as novelty erasers. Until recently, most specialized carving materials could only be purchased by mail order or catalog. These days, it's getting easier to find carving materials in craft stores. Although there are slight differences between different types and brands, you can be sure that they are all "carvable." Experiment with different types, develop your own preferences, and decide which materials work best for specific projects. Check the Resources section on page 79 for more information.

Small, soft, white vinyl erasers can be found at art or office supply stores. You can also use inexpensive novelty erasers made of similar material in fun shapes (available at discount or gift stores, or novelty mail-order catalogs). Even the eraser on the end of a pencil can be carved into a tiny image and used as a stamp or to create a nice, large dot.

If you'd like to carve a bigger block, try carving material often called "student carving material," available from school art supply catalogs. Some types have a coloring agent added to make it easier to see your carved lines or even a wood grain texture to make your finished carving look like a wood carving.

There are many other sources, large and small, from which you can order material by mail or on the Internet.

White vinyl erasers

Here are some ways to evaluate a carving material to see if it suits your carving style:

- When selecting material, make sure there are no bubbles or defects that can interfere with your carving strokes and cause bloopers in your carving. If you do find flaws in your block, cut them out or plan your design around them.

- Check the density of the material. Soft squishy material is very easy to carve, and works well for fine lines and details. Dense, rubbery carving material also holds a finely-cut line well. If your blades are well-sharpened, you can achieve good results carving fine lines in this material.

- Consider the thickness of the material. You can save money by carving on both sides of a carving block, so a thick block can be a good choice (if the material is dense enough, you can also do this with thinner sheets).

- Some older brands of carving material are made from a substance which looks smooth and creamy but may crumble and break, causing unpredictable carving lines. Its coarse grainy texture makes it hard to carve smoothly, and your stamp will disintegrate almost immediately after you finish carving it. Some people like this crumbly quality for the edginess it gives their stamps.

BEYOND TRADITIONAL MATERIALS

Carvers often experiment with "found rubber," such as plumbing gasket rubber (found in plumbing supply stores), scraps of red rubber from commercial rubber stamps, and even baked sheets of polymer clay. Once you're comfortable with traditional materials, give some of these and other unusual materials a try.

PREPARING MATERIAL FOR CARVING

Some brands of carving material are smooth on both sides, while others have a smooth side and a slightly nubbly textured side. You may develop a preference for carving on one side or the other, but it's OK to carve on either side. If you're using an eraser with a logo or raised lettering, use a fine-grit sandpaper to lightly sand and smooth the surface.

CUTTING YOUR MATERIAL

It costs less to buy large sheets of carving material and cut them into more manageable pieces than it does to buy smaller blocks.

To cut a sheet of carving material, use a metal straightedge or ruler, a small mat-cutting or craft knife, and a cutting mat to protect your work surface.

Decide where you want to cut either by measuring and marking a line with a pencil, or simply by adjusting the straightedge to the position you choose. Hold the straightedge firmly on the carving material with one hand, and draw the knife gently but firmly along the edge with your other hand (see photo below). Make several cuts until you've cut all the way through the carving material, rather than through the entire thickness all at once.

If you want to cut small pieces of material, cut about halfway through and snap it apart by bending and flexing along the cut line (this works better for some brands than others).

Cutting a vinyl eraser with a straightedge and craft knife

OTHER MATERIALS

For transferring images (see pages 12–13), you'll need a pencil and tracing paper or vellum (available at art, craft, or office supply stores). If you want to try acetone transfers, you'll need acetone-based nail polish remover (see Transfer Techniques, page 13). You'll also want an ink pad (usually in a light color) and scrap paper close by so you can check your progress as you work.

Carving Tools

The most common tool for carving stamps is a linoleum gouge (*not* a wood gouge), available at art or craft supply stores in the printmaking section. Linoleum gouges have a short, thick handle made of wood or plastic, and removable V-tip or U-tip blades. These blades, viewed end on, have two cutting edges—both sides of the V and the U. You can use these blades to create very thin, fine lines or very broad, bold lines. You can buy a gouge handle in a set with six different cutting blades or buy handles and blades separately. If you buy a plastic gouge handle, you can unscrew the end and store your blades inside it.

A #1 blade is a very tiny V-shaped blade. The #2 blade has a wider and deeper V-shape. The #3 blade is a deep but narrow U shape, and #4 and #5 are respectively wide and wider U shapes. Some people prefer to use one side or the other of the V or U-tip blade because they can see their carving cut better on one side than on the other. There is no right or wrong side—develop your own preferences.

Most of the stamps in this book were carved with two or three basic blades: the smallest V-shaped blade (#1) and larger and wider U-shaped blade (either the #4 or #5 blade). Starting out, you should have at least one gouge handle and two blades—a #1 and a #5 blade. I don't recommend the #2 blade for your first carving efforts—the blade cuts very deeply and can be hard to control.

Another tool option is a craft knife with a #11 blade. A craft knife usually has a removable, long, triangular-shaped blade with a single cutting edge and a very sharp point. This tool is used to cut carving blocks down to size. It's also useful for getting into very tight corners or establishing a carving guideline for extremely fine lettering and detail lines. Use the tip of the blade to make small cuts in the carving material, then pick out the material as you go. The blade is very sharp—handle with care!

Carving tools from other hobbies are often useful for carving rubber stamps. Try micro-tools (tiny carving tools borrowed from model builders) or cuticle trimmers. An ordinary pin, when pushed gently straight into the carving surface, will leave a round unprinted dot. Small tubes, such as the metal ink tube from a pen, will cut a perfect small circle in material. Poke a circle with the tube and carve around the cut line. You can also use the tube to pull out a round "plug" of material. Check carving web sites on the Internet (see Resources, page 79) for more information on unusual sources for tools and materials.

Keep a straightedge or metal-edged ruler on hand for measuring and cutting material, as well as scissors and a cutting mat. You'll need a sharp, soft lead pencil (denoted by a "B" on the pencil, such as 4B) for drawing or transferring images to your carving block. If you have one, a light box can be useful to help you trace images. For extra-large stamps, you may want to get a very small printing press with a cushioned printing bed, roughly 8 x 8 inches (20.3 x 20.3 cm). Tabletop models are relatively inexpensive, and can save wear and tear on your wrists and fingers (see Inking and Stamping on pages 22–23 for more information).

FROM BOTTOM TO TOP: Sandpaper, craft knives, gouges, assortment of blades, scissors, sharpening stones, poking implements, brayer, ruler, pencil

SHARPENING BLADES

When you're learning to carve, nothing is more frustrating than working with dull blades. Carving material is so soft that your blades may rarely need sharpening, but if you find that they're dull, you can restore the edges with a fine-grade sharpening stone and a drop or two of sharpening oil (or any non-food grade oil).

To sharpen a blade on a sharpening stone, apply a drop or two of oil to the stone. If you're using a sharpening stone meant to be used with water, soak the stone in water briefly instead. Note the angle of the cutting edge of your blade. Hold your gouge so that the angle aligns parallel with the surface of the stone and gently stroke forward into the cutting edge of the stone, or swirl the blade in small circles. For a curved U-shaped gouge, gently turn the blade as you stroke—the movement should trace a figure like a comma. You'll be sharpening the entire face of the U, especially the "legs" which cut into your material. For the V-shaped blade, sharpen both outside edges of the V. Continue until you have the desired sharpness—a dozen or so strokes should do it. Wipe the oil off the blade and test on a scrap piece of material.

Selecting Images for Carving

Now that you've got your materials and tools ready, what are you going to carve? For your very first carving efforts, start with simple images with few details, such as leaves, stars, hearts, birds, or flowers. You can draw and design your own images, but don't worry if you're unsure about your drawing skills. Carving has a way of "bumping up" the quality of a hand-drawn image, so even if your drawing is rough or simple, the quality of your stamped image will appear to be more artistic.

Start a file or envelope for storing interesting visuals and ideas you come across. Whenever you find an intriguing motif, clip and save it. Carving will help you look at the world with new eyes, and you'll find images to carve everywhere!

Look at children's craft or coloring books, inexpensive nature guides (for images of insects, leaves, birds, and animals), newspapers, magazines, and flower and seed catalogs. Stencils also work nicely: instead of painting in the open spots, trace them onto your carving block, then carve away all the background material. A clip art book, filled with copyright-free images, can be a gold mine of ideas. Check postcards, junk mail, ads in the phone book, dictionary illustrations, candy wrappers, wrapping paper, and even children's doodles for motifs. You can also carve images from photographs you've taken.

Transfer Techniques

There are several different ways of getting an image onto your carving block. Your approach to transferring images is entirely up to you. Some people spend a lot of time drawing, tracing, and transferring an image, penciling in every area to be left uncarved. This method takes more preparation time, but leaves much less to be decided once carving begins. There are no design decisions to make—you just carve what isn't penciled.

I don't spend much time on preparation. I usually construct an outline of the image, with detail lines penciled in, and jump right into the carving. I tend to carve very quickly and intuitively, making decisions as I go along. This style obviously results in a lot of goofs for me, but this is my working style, and it suits me.

No matter whether you're a "planner" or a "carve-on-the-fly" type, get comfortable with your personal style. There is simply no right or wrong way to do this stuff, just what works for *you*!

Keep in mind, too, that carving rubber stamps, like printmaking, requires a slight shift in thinking before you start out. If you draw an image directly onto your carving block, it will print backwards from the way you drew it. This is especially important when you're carving letters. A "c" carved directly onto the block will print backwards.

Here are some methods to try. Since carving materials vary in their composition, you'll have to experiment to see which methods work best with which materials.

PHOTO 1

PHOTO 2a

PHOTO 2b

DRAWING ON A BLOCK

Draw an image directly on the carving block with a pencil. Mark only areas meant to be left uncarved; that is, areas darkened by your pencil will also print "dark" when the image is inked and stamped. Remember, that your image will print "backwards" from the way you draw it. You'll remove all the "white" material that is unmarked by the pencil (see photo 1).

DRAW, TRACE, AND BURNISH

Draw or trace the image you want to carve onto a piece of vellum or tracing paper (see photo 2a). Lay the tracing paper on top of your carving block, image side down. Rub the back of the paper with a blunt tool (such as the back of a spoon or your fingernail) to burnish the pencil markings onto your carving block (see photo 2b). Lift the paper to see if the image transferred completely. If it didn't, line up the tracing paper with the image and scratch the area again, or pencil in the missed areas. An image transfered to the block this way will print with the same orientation as the original image (see photo 2c).

This is a good method to use when you want to reuse an image. You simply retrace the image when you need it. One disadvantage of this method is that you will be working with a second-generation image, not the actual image itself—details can be lost.

PHOTO 2c. Left: Image drawn directly on block
Right: Image traced and burnished on block

ACETONE TRANSFER

Make a photocopy or print an image from your computer. Use acetone (or acetone-based nail polish remover) to transfer it to the carving block. The acetone transfers ink from the printed image directly to the block. Freshly printed images produce better results. Cut out the image and place it print-side down on your carving block. Gently dab a little acetone on the back of the paper with a cotton-tipped swab. Don't rub—use just enough acetone to dampen the paper (see photo 3a). Lift a corner of the copy paper and check to see if the image has transferred (see photo 3b). If it hasn't, try repeating the acetone dab (be careful though—too much acetone will dissolve and smear the ink).

With this transfer method, you get a very detailed transfer of your original, so you can carve the image more accurately and consistently. However, you'll need to experiment with different kinds of acetone-based nail polish removers, printer inks, and carving materials to find out which ones work together. Some non-acetone-based removers work, too. Some carving materials are not affected by the acetone, while others immediately become brittle and difficult to carve. Remember that acetone is an extremely volatile material. Read the product safety precautions carefully.

HEAT TRANSFER

Make a photocopy or print an image from your computer printer. Cut out your image, and place it print-side down on the carving block. Use a blank piece of paper between your iron and the carving material to protect your iron. With your iron set on a low setting (the one for synthetic material), lightly iron the image onto the block (see photo 4). You can also use a tacking iron (available from art and craft supply stores or mail-order catalogs). Use higher heat if your image won't transfer at that setting, but don't let the iron get too hot; you may scorch the paper and burn the block. After ironing the paper, lift one corner a bit and see if the image has transferred (see photo 3b).

As with other methods, experiment with your carving block material first, as some respond to this method better than others.

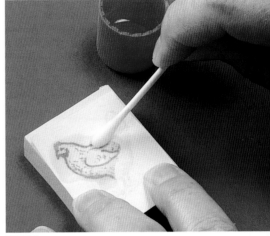

PHOTO 3a

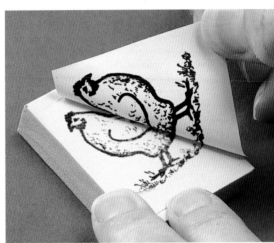

PHOTO 3b

PHOTO 4

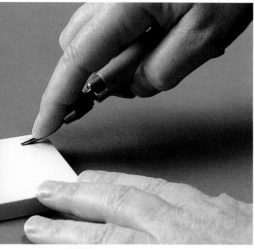

PHOTO 5

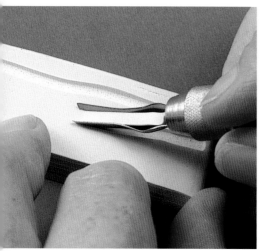

PHOTO 6

Carving Basics

If I could say only three words to the beginning carver, they would be "Shallow, Shallow, Shallow!" Carving too deeply is the single biggest mistake that new carvers make. Not only is it unnecessary to carve deeply, it's frustrating, and results in broken and chipped carvings.

Carve with shallow strokes, especially when you're starting out. You only need to remove a tiny bit of carving material to get an image. Experiment and see for yourself. Even when you're carving out background material, it's best to remove a shallow layer first, then go back and remove another layer if desired.

HOLDING THE GOUGE

Holding your gouge properly will help you to carve correctly. There are two ways to do it. The first method (the way I hold it), is to hold the gouge in your working hand as you would a pencil, at roughly a 30° angle. Hold the carving block on your work surface with your other hand. To carve, just touch the gouge blade to the surface of the carving block, applying enough pressure to break through the "skin." Stroke away from yourself with a smooth relaxed movement, skimming just below the surface of the material (see photo 5).

The second way is to hold the gouge in the palm of your hand with your index finger resting lightly on the blade tip (see photo 6). This technique works best for making very tiny, short, shallow cuts to add detail and shadow effects. Try both ways and see which way works best for you.

CHECKING YOUR PROGRESS

Here's an easy way to check if you're carving too deeply. Look at the curl of vinyl that you leave in your wake as you carve. If you're holding your gouge correctly, both sides of your V-tip or U-tip blade should cut smoothly through the vinyl, and this curl should have a clean-cut edge on both sides. If one or both sides are ragged or breaking, then one or both sides of your blade cutting edges are dipping so far below the surface that they aren't slicing through the top any-more—they are burrowing. You're no longer carving, you're excavating (see photo 7)! Stop, pull out the gouge, and again go back to shallow strokes. If you have trouble getting the gouge blade to break the block surface, or if it seems like the block is very rubbery, your gouge blade may need sharpening.

As you become more experienced, feel free to break the rules, and carve more deeply. When you're more comfortable with carving, you'll have much more control over your carving strokes. Then you can use all the big, bold, deep strokes you want!

Take time to stop and admire your carving progress often. This also helps you catch and correct any areas that don't look right.

Stamp your image on scrap paper with a light-colored ink (so you don't cover any pencil guidelines on your block) as you carve. This helps your eye "see" the image better. If you need to trim down a line or add more white space, it's easy to make these little adjustments as you go along. You might also try keeping a small mirror handy—looking at the image reversed (it will be how the image will print) helps your eye spot mistakes and trouble spots.

Don't worry about perfection. You'll get better with practice! Almost any mistake you make can be corrected, incorporated, or camouflaged.

PHOTO 7

Carving Techniques

STRAIGHT LINES

Practice making straight lines with the large and small gouges on scrap pieces of carving material. Note how finely you can stroke and still get a visible line with the small V-tip blade. Small blades make thin delicate lines. Next, try the U-tip blade. Medium and large U-tip blades make wider, bolder lines (see photo 8). Experiment until you're comfortable with different blades. Start with shallow strokes. You can vary the width of your line by how deeply you carve with the blade.

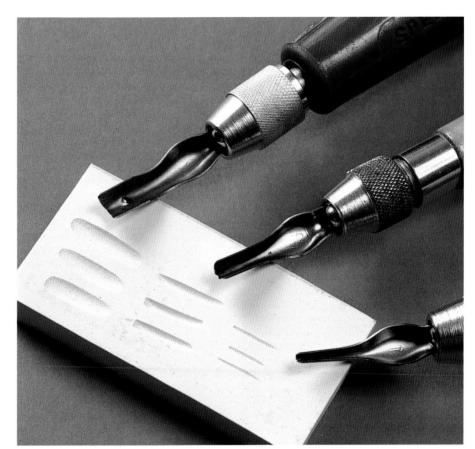

PHOTO 8

TURNING CORNERS AND CURVED LINES

Beginning carvers often make the mistake of twisting and turning the gouge to go around corners and curves. This makes it difficult to maintain and control your cutting edge, and the motion is hard on your hands and wrists. A better way to carve along a curved line is to move or rotate the carving block, *not* your carving hand! Hold your gouge steady in a single position, and apply slight pressure to start the carving line. With your other hand, move the carving block in a smooth, controlled manner. As you carve, turn the block whichever direction you need to (see photos 9a and 9b). Now you can carve every angle and curve with the same pressure and control throughout. It's a safer way to carve, too—you constantly carve *away* from yourself. Practice tighter and tighter turns as you get more proficient with this technique.

PHOTO 9a

PHOTO 9b

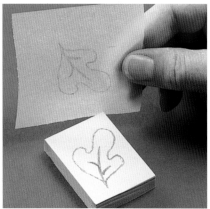

PHOTO 10

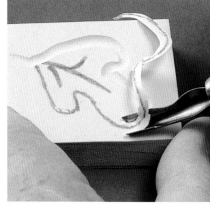

PHOTO 11a

PHOTO 11b

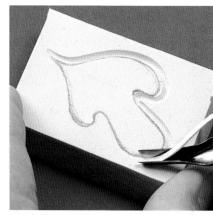

PHOTO 12a

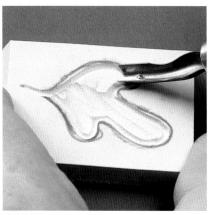

PHOTO 12b

PHOTO 12c

POSITIVE AND NEGATIVE IMAGES

When evaluating new designs to carve, you have to choose which areas will be white and which will be dark. There are no hard and fast rules about this process. A lot of it is simply "artistic interpretation." One image can be carved in many different ways, and all of them may be successful carvings.

NEGATIVE LINE IMAGES

A negative line image is a line that 'prints' as white on a dark background. Pencil on paper makes a dark line on a white background. Carving on a block makes a white line on a dark background. To create a negative line image, draw, or trace and transfer an image onto your carving block (see photo 10). Remember, if you draw directly on the carving block, your printed image will be reversed. For a large, bold image, use the large U-tip gouge. For a smaller or more detailed image, use the small V-tip gouge. Follow the penciled line with your gouge. Carve right on the line, rotating the carving block as you go (see photo 11a). This carved line, when printed, will read as white on a dark background (see photo 11b).

SOLID NEGATIVE IMAGES

A solid negative image prints as a solid white image on a dark background. Draw or transfer the image to your block. Use a large U-tip gouge to scoop out all the carving material from *inside* your image (see photos 12a, 12b, and 12c).

SOLID POSITIVE IMAGES

A solid positive image is a solid image that prints dark on a white background. Again, start with a carved line, but carve along the outside of the image. Remove all the background material outside the outline (see photo 13a). This leaves a solid printed image in an unprinted (white) background—a positive image. Adding a few fine-carved detail lines (which will show as white in the stamped image) will add interest to the stamp (see photo 13b).

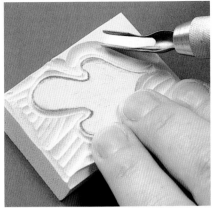

PHOTO 13a

PHOTO 13b

POSITIVE LINE IMAGES

You can also create an image that prints the way a drawing looks—that is, the *lines* of your design will print and appear dark on a white background. To get lines to print, carve everything away *but* the lines you've drawn. In other words, you will carve two guidelines: one along the inside of your penciled line, and one along the outside, and then remove all the background material inside and outside your penciled line.

Draw, or trace and transfer a penciled image to your block. Carve around the outside of the penciled line.

Now go back and position the small V-tip gouge just *inside* the penciled line. Carve along the inside of the entire image (see photo 14a). Carve around any detail lines in the same manner (see photo 14b). Use a large U-tip gouge to remove all background material outside the guideline. Do the same for the material inside the guidelines (see photo 14c).

Your image will be defined by an uncarved outline (see photo 14d). This creates a totally different look for your carved images. With a little practice, you'll be able to carve very closely along your pencil lines.

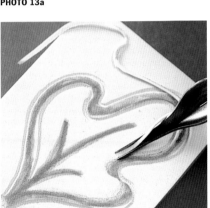

PHOTO 14a

PHOTO 14b

PHOTO 14c

PHOTO 14d

OUTLINING

When carving around a penciled guideline, you can create a bolder image by leaving your carved outlines wider, or create a more delicate line by carving very close to your guidelines. Lines that are perfectly consistent in thickness look like printed lines; lines with varied thickness can look like brushstrokes.

Carving Choices

Throughout the carving process you'll make decisions about how you want your printed image to appear. Let's say you're carving an image of a chicken, for example. There are several different ways you can approach your project.

With a solid image of a chicken, you can indicate a wing by creating a simple carved detail line (see photo 15a). Another option is to carve along the inside of your guideline and carve out the material inside the chicken, but leave a solid area uncarved to indicate your wing and a tiny dot uncarved as an eye (see photo 15b). To create a chicken that prints totally as an outline (see photo 15c), you can indicate a wing by leaving only a carved outline for the wing (rather than a completely solid wing).

PHOTO 15a

PHOTO 15b

Shadowing Techniques

Shadowing is another technique for adding depth and detail to your carved image. You have three different options for creating shadows: solid, line shadows, and crosshatching. Experiment with the different styles by carving a simple object, like an apple.

PHOTO 16a

SOLID SHADOW

Create a solid shadow by leaving the "shadowed" areas solid black. To do this, determine where you want your light and shadow areas to be, and leave the shadow area uncarved (see photo 16a)

LINE SHADOW

To create a shadow area with lines (gradations of light and darkness), start with a solid shadow, then add lines with your gouge to temper the amount of darkness in the shadow. Remember that you are shading the opposite way as you would with a pencil; when drawing, you add darkness by adding lines, but when carving you add light/whiteness by adding carved lines. The more lines you carve, the lighter that area will read.

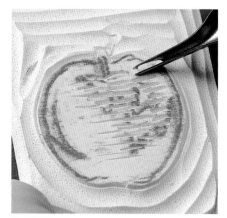

PHOTO 16b

PHOTO 15c

Plan where you want your shadows, and work from darker areas (less carving) to lighter areas (more carving). At the point where the shadow area starts, carve very shallow, widely spaced lines. Move across the shadow and add light by carving more closely spaced lines. At the lightest part of the shadow, carve everything away (see photos 16b and 16c).

PHOTO 16c

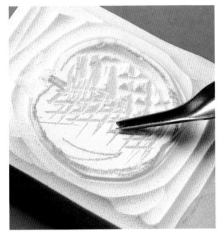
PHOTO 17a

CROSS-HATCHING

A third shadowing technique is cross-hatching. Carved lines cross each other, creating a pattern like woven cloth. The more you lines you carve, the lighter that area will be. Start creating a few widely spaced lines at your darkest shadow area, then cross over these lines with more lightly carved lines (see photos 17a and 17b). Your pattern will look like woven fabric. Proceed across the rest of your shadow, creating more and more lines, making the areas lighter and lighter. Go slowly at first. Remember, you can always carve away a little more material, but you can't put it back!

PHOTO 17b

Borders

Creating a border for a carved image adds a powerful design element to your stamp. It's one of my favorite ways to give a stamp more visual punch.

SOLID BORDER

Carve a straight line (thick or thin) just inside the edge of your carving block to create a solid printed border (see photo 18). Use your straightedge if you want a perfectly straight and even line.

HAND-HEWN LOOK

Another alterative is to use a large U-tip gouge to remove all background material up to $\frac{1}{8}$ inch (3 mm) or so from the edge of the stamp, leaving irregular scoop marks just inside the edge (see photo 19). This gives your stamp a rustic "hand-hewn" look.

DASHED LINE

To make a solid border into a dashed line, cut guidelines with your small V-tip gouge or craft knife, mark off small spaces at regular intervals, then remove the material in between the guidelines (see photo 20). Use this technique to create a long, dashed line, or a thick "picket fence" line (see photo 21). Both are effective borders.

PHOTO 18

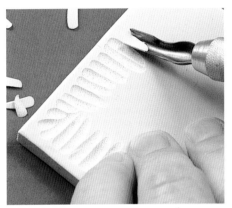
PHOTO 19

PHOTO 20

PHOTO 21

PHOTO 22

PHOTO 23

PHOTO 24

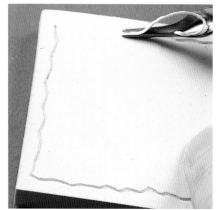

PHOTO 25

DOTTED BORDER

To create dots that will print white on a dark border, carve a thick, solid border. Next, use a pin or other sharp pointed tool to make regular indentations in the border (see photo 22). Bigger tools will result in larger dots.

ZIGZAG BORDER

To create a zigzag border, draw a guideline with the small V-tip gouge, then carve around this guideline (see photo 23).

POSTAGE STAMP BORDER

For a postage stamp border, pencil in two parallel guidelines along the edge of the block. The inside border will stay uncarved. On the outer border, make small, regular scoop cuts to create the look of perforations. Line up the gouge tip against the outside penciled line, carving out to the edge of the block. Punch out U-shaped scoops. Use a large U-tip gouge for large, thick perforations, and a smaller one for smaller perforations (see photo 24).

DECKLED BORDER

For an artfully deckled border, simply draw a randomly squiggled line about $1/16$ to $1/8$ inch (1.6 to 3 mm) inside the outer edge of the block. Carve along this guideline (see photo 25).

Design and Composition

You could fill an entire book discussing the theory of design and composition, but I'll stick to reviewing simple techniques for modifying and adapting an image for carving.

PHOTO 26a

PHOTO 26b

PHOTO 27a

BACKGROUND AND ACCENT IMAGES

A simple design trick is to complement your stamped image with a background image (created on a different piece of carving material). Create an interesting pattern or motif and stamp it in a subtle, light-colored, or neutral ink, then stamp your featured image on top of it.

A background image may consist of simple vertical or horizontal detail lines (wiggly or straight) or both combined to create a "woven fabric" look (see photos 26a and 26b). Use a pointed tool to create white dots on a solid background. Carve a positive or negative image of a spiral (see photos 27a and 27b). This can be especially subtle carved in very fine lines.

Another versatile design element is an accent stamp, a smaller version of the background stamp used to highlight a spot on your printed carved image. Stars, zigzags, and spirals are useful motifs (see photo 28).

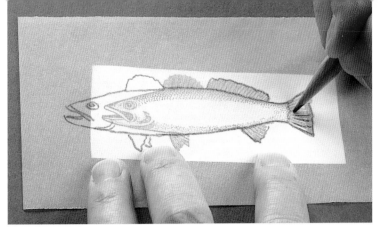

PHOTO 29

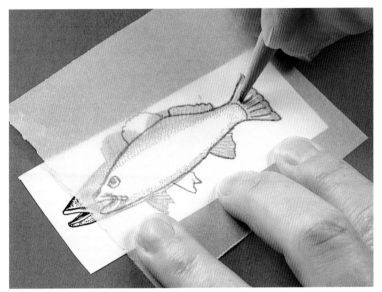

PHOTO 30

PHOTO 27b

PHOTO 28

ADDING DESIGN ELEMENTS OR ALTERING AN IMAGE

Keep this in mind: you don't have to create an entire composition on one stamp. You can combine several single images to achieve the composition you want. Single images can be more versatile because they can be combined in many ways. A fish postage stamp is a fish postage stamp, but a fish image can be used inside a stamp border, in a river, in a fish bowl, or stamped in multiples to create a school of fish.

You can also design a complex composition in stages. If you use the tracing paper/burnishing method to transfer images to your carving block, you'll find it easy to modify and adapt your designs.

If you love a certain fish image, but its fin is too small or fussy to carve in the outline style, leave it uncarved to print solid, or add only a few detail lines. If you want a longer fish, "extend" its body by moving your tracing paper and drawing a little extra length in (see photo 29). Shorten the image by moving the paper to "skip over" and leave out a section of the body (see photo 30). If you want a more dramatic eye, draw it larger on your tracing paper. If you don't like an element you've modified, simply erase it. When you have modified the image to your satisfaction, transfer the final image to the carving block.

Add separate elements to your design by tracing them on separate sheets of tracing paper, then position and transfer them where you want them on the block. When you trace your image, you can decide as you go whether to leave out details, features, or shadows, add them in with your pencil, or modify an entire image.

Inking and Stamping

Use regular ink pads for your carved stamps (see photo 31). Pads are available with either pigment inks (opaque and thick, like gouache or acrylic paint) or dye inks (translucent to transparent, like watercolor). Acid-free inks will help prolong the life of your carved stamps and your stamped images.

To ink, lightly tap or squish (never pound or press) your carved stamp on the ink pad, and check to make sure that it's evenly inked. An ink pad with a raised pad is more flexible than an inset pad because you can use it to ink a stamp that's actually larger than the pad.

For larger stamps, or when working with inks or paints in tubes, you can use a brayer (a handheld roller) to ink a stamp. This doesn't work with thicker paints and inks, as the thick paint can clog up your carved lines. If this happens, an alternative is to squirt a very small amount of paint onto a smooth surface, such as a pane of glass or piece of clear acrylic. Roll the brayer in the ink until it's evenly coated and the ink is "tacky" (see photo 32). Roll the brayer across the printing surface of your carved stamp (see photo 33).

You can also ink a stamp with special marking pens made for coloring commercial stamps. Color the stamp itself with the pens. This allows you to separately color individual areas. Follow the manufacturer's instructions for using these pens.

Once you've inked the stamp, set it gently onto your paper without wriggling or moving it. Apply even pressure all over the back of the stamp with your hands or fingertips. Lift the stamp and look for areas that didn't print fully (see photo 34). If some didn't, repeat the process and make sure your ink pad isn't dried out and that your printing surface is flat and even.

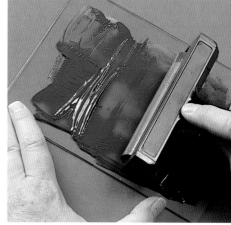

PHOTO 32

PHOTO 33

PHOTO 31

PHOTO 34

Because hand-carved stamps are made from soft, flexible material, it's possible that carved-out areas will actually be pushed far enough down onto the paper to print. This may result in small cut lines that show where your gouge carved away excess material. If you don't want these lines to show, go back and carve out these areas some more to clean them up. I keep the lines in because they add movement and energy to the printed image.

Unlike commercial red rubber stamps which are sold mounted on blocks of wood, hand-carved stamps usually don't need to be mounted. You can add extra support to large stamps or thin carving materials by positioning something sturdy and flat across the back of the stamp while you're stamping. Try using a book, small cutting board, or a piece of wood cut to size for this purpose. Lay the object on top of the block, press firmly down, and remove it carefully after stamping so as not to smudge your inked image. This method will allow you to apply even pressure across the back of the stamp.

Another option, especially useful when working with large stamps, is to use a small tabletop printing press like those made to work with linoleum block printing (see photo 35). A press is relatively inexpensive and can be ordered by mail or online from art supply companies. To use a press, lay the paper you wish to stamp on the cushioned printing bed, and position your carved stamp on it. Lower the handle to apply gentle pressure (see photo 36). Raise the handle, carefully lift the stamp, and remove your printed paper. With this method, you use less pressure to get an evenly stamped print, and it's much easier on your hands and wrists.

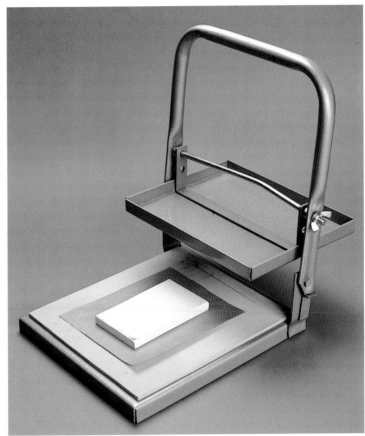

PHOTO 35

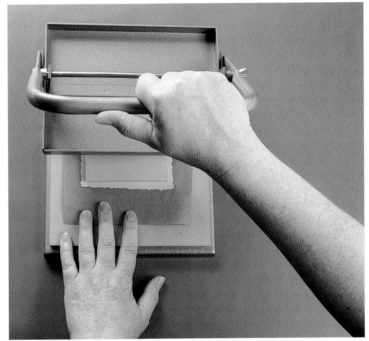

PHOTO 36

Cleaning

Many stampers only clean enough ink off their stamps to keep from transferring one color ink to another color ink pad, while others scrub them religiously after each use. The choice is purely personal. If you want very clean stamps, be sure to wash them as soon as possible after using them, as some inks are harder to remove than others. Old ink is much, much harder to remove than fresh ink.

You can clean your stamps with ordinary soap and water. Simply moisten a few sheets of paper towel and fold them into a pad, add a drop or two of soap or dishwashing liquid (not *dishwasher* detergent), and daub off your stamps (see photo 37). Ordinary baby wipes are also a good solution for cleaning stamps. Just fold

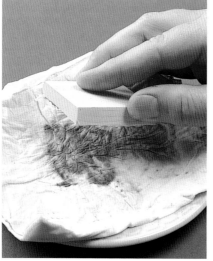

PHOTO 37

one into a square and tap your stamp on the wipe a few times until it stamps clean on the wipe, then let it air-dry. You can repeat this process periodically as you work. The wipe will work for many cleanings, even when it looks very inky.

You can also use commercial stamp cleaners. Most of these are made for regular red rubber stamps, though, so test any cleaners first on a scrap of carving material. A gentle plastic scrubber will also help the cleaning. If you use solvents or powerful commercial cleaning products, test them on a scrap of carving material first. Some solvents, like acetone, seem to have no effect on the stamps at first, but damage can show up later, especially if the solvent is not completely removed after use.

Storing Your Images

Carving material is pretty durable stuff but you may want to take some simple precautions in storing your stamps to ensure you'll get years of enjoyment from them.

Stamps should be stored in a dust-free area, out of direct sunlight and away from temperature extremes. Stamps stored touching each other may eventually stick to each other. Keep them separate or wrap them individually in blank newsprint, wax paper, or parchment paper or arrange the stamps in layers, making sure they don't touch each other, and cover each layer with a sheet of blank paper.

Stamps can pick up the surface texture of anything you store them on (bare wood, for example), and "pull" the ink from printed newsprint or colored papers. Some carving material reacts to styrene plastic (the hard, clear, glass-like plastic sometimes used in storage boxes). Line any storage

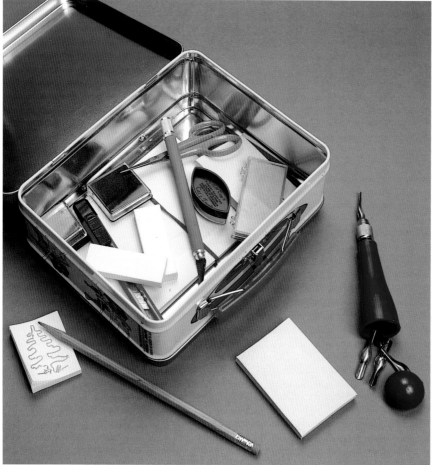

PHOTO 38

PHOTO 39

Recording and Sharing Your Images

Last but not least, treat yourself to a little blank book, journal, or a simple notebook, and use it to record your stamp images. As I carve a new stamp, I stamp the image in a little blank journal with handmade paper sheets (see photo 39). You may want to date your images and write little notes about where you found the image, what techniques you used, and so on. It's a good way to keep track of all your images, record new techniques, and jot down ideas for future projects. Be sure to go through your book periodically and admire your progress with your carving techniques.

Share your images with friends and family. If you're an experienced stamper, you may already enjoy making cards and stamp-decorated accessories and participating in artist swaps and mail art projects. If you're new to stamping, a wonderful world of color, creative carving, and fun awaits you. Carving your own stamps offers you a whole new dimension of creativity. Only one warning—carving rubber stamps is highly addictive, but fortunately, calorie-free!

container you use with clean sheets of newsprint, aluminum foil, or baking parchment. Stamps aren't normally breakable (most simply bounce if dropped), but some very soft carving materials dent easily. They'll hold up better with careful handling.

At first, you'll probably be able to contain your carved stamp collection in any kind of box—a cigar box, a wooden box, a plastic container, etc. As your collection grows, get creative with your storage ideas. Try office supply stores, craft stores, yard sales, flea markets, hardware stores or office supply stores for storage containers. I use a set of cardboard storage cubes, each with three cardboard drawers. Plastic carts (the kind available at many office supply and discount stores) with see-through drawers can tuck away into a closet or under a worktable, and be wheeled out quickly when you're ready to work. Tool organizers from hardware stores, or old

dental cabinets are also wonderful for storing supplies.

Some other alternatives are cardboard pizza boxes, candy boxes, wooden wine crates, cassette and video tape holders, an old suitcase or a picnic basket with a lid. Just be careful your carving blocks don't come into contact with the wicker weave, or you will have wicker-weave imprinted stamps.

Once you get hooked on stamp carving, you may want to make a travel set of carving tools and supplies so you can carve where and whenever you the mood strikes you (see photo 38). A lunch box is the perfect size for stashing a few gouges, a pencil, a few blocks of carving material, transfer paper, and a craft knife. A cigar box with some sort of closure (a large rubber band, a velcro strap, etc.) works nicely, too. Explore your local craft store for other nifty portable containers.

TROUBLESHOOTING

PROBLEM

*Choppy, uneven outline
or raggedy-edged cuts.*

SOLUTION

Check to make sure you aren't
holding the gouge at too high an
angle or cutting too deeply. Make
light, shallow cuts.

SOLUTION

Your gouge blade might be dull. Try
another blade, or sharpen your
blade (see page 11). Carving material is soft, so you shouldn't have to
sharpen your blades very often.

SOLUTION

Examine your carving material. If
it's grainy, brittle, or crumbly, then
your carving lines won't be smooth.
Either incorporate the graininess
into your design, or switch to a
product with smoother consistency.

PROBLEM

*You've accidentally cut into an
outline and left a small gouge.*

SOLUTION

Use either a fine gouge or a sharp
craft knife to cut a smooth guideline that eliminates the gouge; then
trim along this guideline.

PROBLEM

*You've accidentally cut off
a design element.*

SOLUTION

Decide if the error can be ignored,
replaced, fixed with a marker pen,
or changed. For example, if you're
carving a bee and cut off one of its
legs, you could:

- Carve away the rest of the leg.

- Carve a new leg on a small scrap
  of carving material and stamp
  the new leg after stamping the
  rest of the bee.

If you've cut away part of a border
while carving an image, you could:

- Fill in the missing area with a
  marker pen in the same color as
  your stamp pad ink.

Eyes are often the trickiest element
to carve. Carve the eyes first, right
after you transfer an image. Then, if
they are messed up, you haven't
invested all that time in the rest of
the design. If you do make a
mistake, try carving out the eye
area and leaving it white or:

- Carve out the eye area and then
  use colored pens or markers to
  add the eye detail back in.

PROBLEM

Incomplete image printed.

SOLUTION

Make sure your pad is thoroughly
inked.

SOLUTION

Move the stamp around on the ink
pad, gently tapping it to make sure
it's inked evenly and thoroughly.

SOLUTION

Gently sand the printing surface of
the stamp with an extremely fine-
grit sandpaper (600 and higher
grit) to remove the "shiny" finish
before stamping. This can help
carving material pick up ink more
evenly from the ink pad.

SOLUTION

Press evenly all over the stamping
surface when printing. See Inking
and Stamping on page 22 for more
ideas.

PROBLEM

*Ink has obliterated the details
in the image.*

SOLUTION

Make sure your paper isn't too
glossy to absorb the ink, or too
absorbent. Some papers are so
absorbent, they act like a sponge
when they are printed on. The ink
spreads into the paper quickly,
resulting in a blobby image instead
of a crisp image. Test out several
other papers and see if you get the
same results.

SOLUTION

Make sure the ink or paint you're
using isn't too thick.

SOLUTION

Check the stamp to make sure there
isn't too much ink or paint on it. If
you are working with a water-
soluble ink or paint, try adding a
bit of water, or inking more lightly.

SOLUTION

Use a brayer to "ink up" your
surface (see page 22).

PROBLEM

*The cutting lines show in the
stamped image, especially in
the background.*

SOLUTION

Accept this as a quirk of hand-
carved stamps. It's the nature of the
soft and squishy carving material.

SOLUTION

Ease up on the pressure you apply
to stamp.

SOLUTION

Continue carving away at these
lines until the stamp image area is
left higher than the background.

RUBBER STAMP PROJECTS

Carving material,
roughly 2 x 3 inches
(5.1 x 7.6 cm)

Pencil

Small V-tip gouge

Large U-tip gouge

Craft knife (optional)

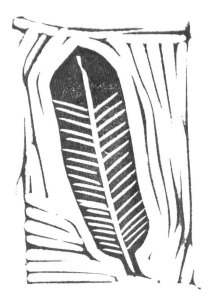

Feather

This design is very easy to sketch and quick to carve. These instructions are for a feather about 2¾ inches (6.9 cm) long, but you can adapt this image to any size you need. In fact, by using the same construction technique and altering the outline of the image, you can also quickly carve a simple leaf.

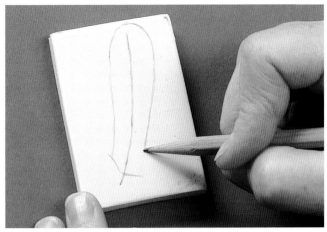

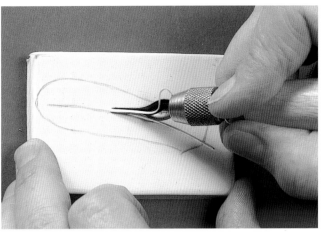

1 Sketch a rough outline in the shape of a feather—slightly narrower at the base, widening a bit at the top. Your image should be a little less than 2¾ inches (6.9 cm) long. Draw a guideline down the center of your feather.

2 Carve a thick line right on the central guideline with the small V-tip gouge. Try to taper it at the top.

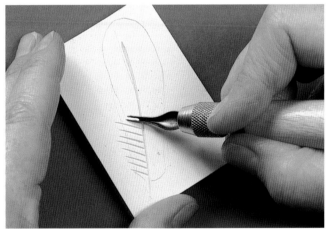

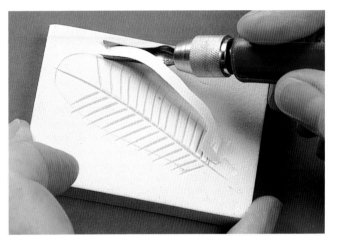

3 Draw a series of parallel ribs at angles off each side of the center line, or carve these ribs freehand. Carve right on your rib guidelines with a small V-tip gouge. Don't worry about making your ribs uniform or the same length, just try to carve the lines roughly parallel to each other. Stop carving ribs a short distance from the top of the center guideline.

4 Carve around your outer guideline with the large U-tip blade. At the bottom of the feather, carve around the stem to outline it.

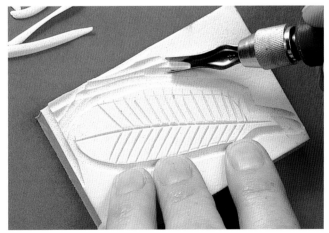

5 Remove the background material from outside your outer guideline with the large U-tip gouge.

Globe Stamp

A delightful little globe stamp can be used to embellish correspondence and packages. It makes an excellent "faux postage" stamp. Highlight any continent or hemisphere you wish. Use your stamp with real postage stamps, as seen here, or stamp your globe image on sticky or gummed paper and use decorative edging scissors to create your own stamp.

1 Draw or trace a circle about 1½ inches (3.8 cm) across. Refer to a world map or globe and sketch in a rough depiction of the countries you wish to portray, or use the globe template on page 78. Don't go for detail—even a very vague land mass will read well. You may want to pencil in these land masses to help you remember to leave them uncarved.

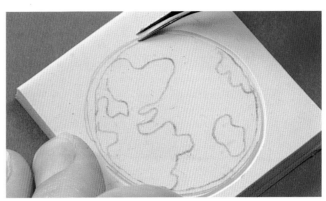

2 Carve around the outside of the penciled circle line with the small V-tip gouge.

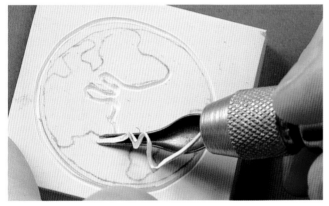

3 Carve around the land masses with the small V-tip gouge. Remember that some of these will merge into the outside circle line.

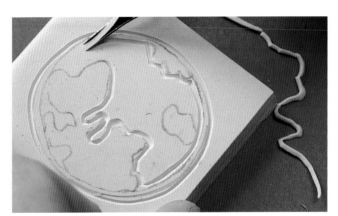

4 Where there is no land mass, carve along the inside of the penciled circle line with the small V-tip gouge.

5 Carve out the large sea areas with the large U-tip gouge.

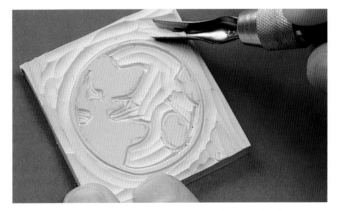

6 Remove all background material outside the outer guideline with the U-tip gouge. If you like, carve a different view of the globe on the back of the stamp. Check your carving with an ink pad in a light color and scrap paper. Make any adjustments as necessary.

Landscape

Simple landscape elements can be combined in different ways to create a variety of scenes. Combine these two stamps to create a mountain beneath the clouds, or use your simple cloud lines to create a green field or a river running in front of your mountain. You can overlap the images if you choose. Add a plain solid circle stamp for a moon or a sun in the upper corner.

YOU WILL NEED

2 blocks of carving material, each in the
size of your choice

Pencil

Large U-tip gouge

Craft knife (optional)

Small V-tip gouge

1 Lightly pencil in a double-mountain shape on a rectangular piece of carving material. Taper the image to a point at both sides.

2 Carve on or along the outside of your outline with the large U-tip gouge.

3 Carve away the background material outside your guideline with a large U-tip gouge, or trim the block with a craft knife.

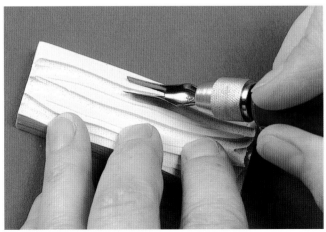

4 Use the large U-tip gouge to create the cloud image on your second block of carving material. Carve very gently wavy lines along the length of the block.

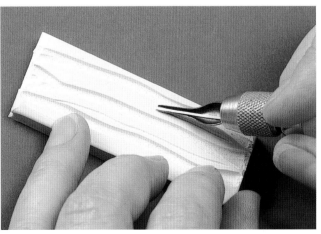

5 You can break up the solid look of these waves by adding slight carving detail with a small V-tip gouge.

Oak Leaves

This oak leaf design looks great stamped around the border of a frame, across a folded plain card, or on the top of stationery. Try making both a solid and an outlined version of this image, each with detail lines. Stamp your leaves with several different autumn-colored inks—gold, russet, brown, or pumpkin. Pair them with an acorn or a squirrel for an autumn theme, or carve a series of different leaves—maple, elm, or birch. Combine smaller versions of your leaves with the oak tree stamp on page 56.

YOU WILL NEED

Carving material, 1½ x 2½ inches
(3.8 x 6.4 cm)

Pencil

Oak leaf template on page 78 (optional)

Tracing paper
(or use the transfer method of your choice)

Small V-tip gouge

Medium U-tip gouge

Large U-tip gouge

1 Draw or trace a leaf shape (use the template on page 78 or the image of your choice) on a small piece of tracing paper, and transfer the image to your carving block.

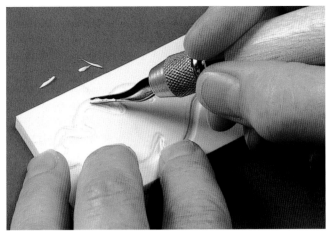

2 Carve along the outside of the penciled guideline with your small V-tip gouge. Keep your carving hand steady, and twist the carving block to carve around the tight turns.

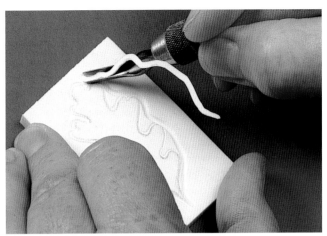

3 With the medium U-tip gouge, carve a rough outline outside the guideline you carved in step 2.

4 Use the small gouge to carve away background material from the tiny "inlet" areas around the leaf image, then continue to carve away background material from the guideline with the large U-tip gouge. Move your gouge away from the leaf image, using a scooping action. Bring the gouge back up to the surface at the end of each carving stroke so that the vinyl doesn't chip or break off. Stop carving about $\frac{1}{16}$ inch (1.6 mm) away from the outer edge of the carving block to create a nice hand-hewn border. If you don't want a border, simply remove all background material around the leaf.

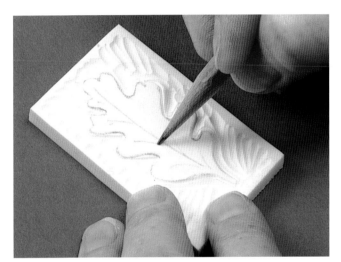

5 Pencil in veins on your leaf.

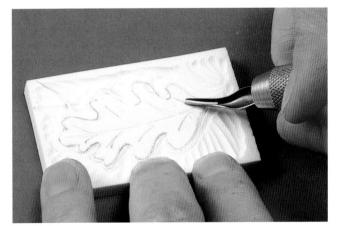

6 Carve out the veins with the small V-tip gouge, carving on the pencil lines, rather than alongside them. Shallow cuts will make delicate veins, slightly deeper cuts will make bolder veins.

Outlined Leaf

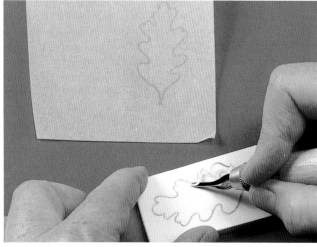

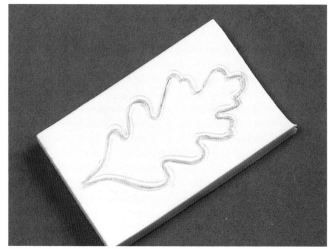

1 Trace and transfer your image, making your penciled line slightly thicker than before. With the small V-tip gouge, carve along the inside of your penciled line.

2 Carve along the outside of this same line using the same small gouge. You can actually carve the inside and outside of this line in reverse order, but it's easier to compensate for mistakes by carving the inside first.

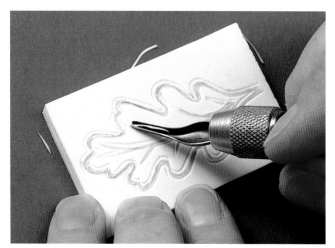

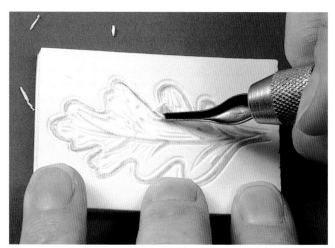

3 Draw veins on the leaf, making the guideline a little thicker than usual. Carve along both sides of the veins with the small V-tip gouge.

4 Carefully carve away the inside of the leaf, being careful not to cut away the vein details. Carve away the background material as you did for the solid leaf.

Fish Post

I love to carve fish! There are plenty of fish images around to work with—this one came from an old pocket fishing guide. If you can't find just the right fish, it's easy to mix and match the parts to make your own unique image. You can also add extra elements to your stamp. For this fish postage stamp, the phrase and number elements were traced on separate sheets of tracing paper, then positioned and transferred to the carving block. Make an entire school of fish posts in different postal denominations!

1 Trace or draw the fish image on the tracing paper (use the template on page 78 or an image of your choice), making any adjustments to the image, if you like. Transfer the image to the carving block by burnishing, or use another transfer method (see pages 12–13).

2 Select the word or phrase you want to appear on the stamp, and trace it onto a piece of tracing paper (*pesce postale* means "fish post" in Italian).

3 Position the word or phrase where you want it, and transfer it onto the carving block. Be sure to leave a bit of room for the border.

4 Trace a number for the postal denomination, if you wish. Position it where you want it on the block, and transfer it.

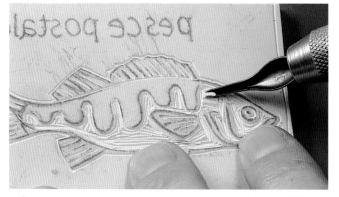

5 Carve a guideline for the thin, solid border about 1/16 inch (1.6 mm) from the edge of the carving block using your small V-tip gouge. Use the same gouge to carve around the fish on the outside of your penciled line.

6 Decide which areas will be left black with detail lines, and which areas will be carved out in outline style. In this stamp, I chose to leave the fins solid with detail lines. Carve the small areas first, especially the fish eye. Carve the inside of the eye first, then carve the guideline on the outside of the eye. Continue to carve away any areas to be left white, such as the insides of the lips, gills, etc.

7 Carve fine detail lines on the solid fins and a detail line along the fish's back.

8 When the fish is done, start in on the letters and number (that way, if the letters don't look good, you can simply carve them out and carve a separate stamp for the postal phrase). Carve the insides of the letters first—the enclosed parts of the letters p, o, e, and a. You can use the craft knife to create a guideline by cutting carefully around the letters first, if you wish, then use your small gouge.

9 With the large U-tip gouge, remove the background material. Use the craft knife or small gouge to get into tight areas. Ink your image and do a test stamp to look for any missed uncarved areas or raggedy letters, then make adjustments as necessary.

VARIATIONS

You can create a perforated border for the stamp instead, or a checkered line. See Borders, page 19, for instructions.

Chick and Egg

It's fun and versatile to carve stamps in sets, such as this chick and egg duo. You can use the images together or separately, placing your chick and egg side by side, or stamping the chick inside the egg. Carve your stamps on opposite sides of the same block to ensure that you always have both images on hand.

1 Trace and transfer an egg shape, or draw it freehand directly on the block. Carve along both sides of the penciled line using a small V-tip gouge. It's a simple line to be carved, no detail!

YOU WILL NEED
2 blocks of carving material, each 1½ x 2 inches (3.8 x 5.1 cm) or 1 thick block
Pencil
Tracing paper (or transfer method of your choice)
Small V-tip gouge
Medium U-tip gouge
Chick template on page 78 (optional)
Craft knife (optional)

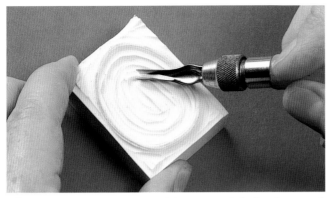

2 Carve away the inside of the egg and the background material outside the egg with the medium U-tip gouge. If you are using the reverse side of the block to carve the chick, do not cut down this block into an egg-shaped stamp. You may cut off the chick!

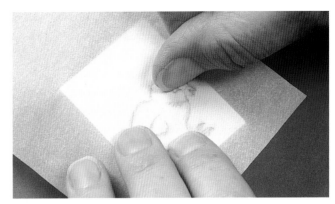

3 Trace or draw an image of a chicken (use the template on page 78 or an image of your choice). It should be small enough to fit inside the egg shape. Transfer the image of the chick to the back of your carving block.

4 Use the small V-tip gouge to make very fine, short strokes roughly perpendicular to your penciled guideline, creating a fuzzy look for your chick. Your strokes don't need to be exactly the same length—you'll be trimming them down later. Add fine fuzzy strokes along the guideline you've drawn for the wings and cheek of the chick.

5 When you've finished with the fuzzy strokes, carve clean lines around the chick's beak and feet with the small V-tip gouge.

6 Carve the eye detail.

7 When your fuzzy strokes are done, carve a new outline just above them with a medium-tip gouge. In effect, you'll be trimming your strokes evenly to about $\frac{1}{16}$ to $\frac{1}{8}$ inch (2 to 3 mm) in length. Carve away the background, then stamp the egg outline, and stamp the chick image inside the egg.

Tall Pine Tree

The long narrow silhouette of a pine tree makes a bold and dramatic statement and really stands out when used as a repeat motif, such as in the forest on this handsome wrapping paper. Stamp your images in greens or black. If you want to show distance between the trees, make the foreground trees darker and the background trees lighter. Add in details with a black fine-tip marker or pen. This stamp also looks great when paired with other landscape elements, such as the images on pages 32 and 46.

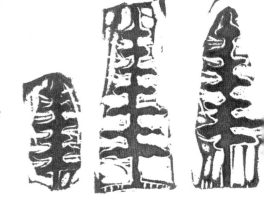

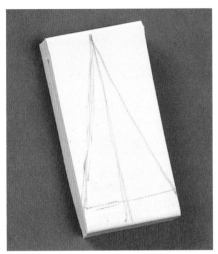 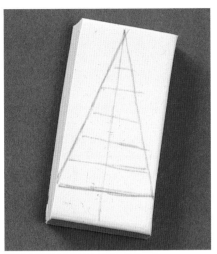 

1 Draw a light pencil line lengthwise down the middle of your carving block. This will be the pine tree trunk. Lightly draw two angled lines down from the top of the trunk (one on each side), ending approximately ⅜ inch (9.5 mm) from the bottom. To create the bottom branch guideline, draw a horizontal line connecting the ends of these two lines. This will create a triangle-shaped area. Your tree branches will fall inside this triangle.

2 Draw six to eight lines, approximately ⅛ inch (3 mm) apart down the length of the triangle. These will be branch guidelines.

3 Starting from the bottom branch guideline and moving out toward the triangular branch guideline, pencil in wriggly tree branches around the branch guidelines. You can also carve freehand around the branch guidelines (as shown in the photo) with a small V-tip gouge. Make sure to stay inside the triangular border guideline as you carve, and rotate the block when you're ready to start carving the branches on the opposite side of the trunk. Don't worry about being exact or about each higher branch being smaller than the one before it. Real pine trees are irregular, too.

YOU WILL NEED

Carving material, ⅞ x 2 inches (2.2 x 5.1 cm)
Pencil
Small V-tip gouge
Large U-tip gouge
Ink pad
Scrap paper

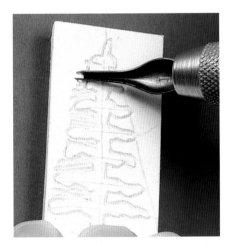 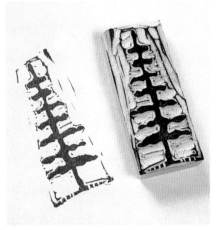

4 When you're done carving the branches, carve away the background material between the branches. Use the small V-tip gouge for small areas and the large U-tip gouge for larger areas.

5 Carve away the background material outside the triangle area, leaving the tree trunk solid. Ink your stamp to check it, then make any adjustments as necessary.

YOU WILL NEED

Carving material,
1¼ x 1¾ inches (3.2 x 4.4 cm)

Pencil

Rabbit template on page 78
(optional)

Tracing material (optional)

Small V-tip gouge

Large U-tip gouge

Ink pad in a light color

Scrap paper

Rabbit

This stamp was carved from very dense carving material, which picks up fine detail lines beautifully. Experiment on scraps of carving material to see how your brand handles such fine carving lines. Pair this rabbit with a simple solid egg shape to turn it into an Easter bunny. Or add a carrot stamp—give your stamp animals something to munch on! Add a few blades of grass with a marking pen or simple carved stamp to transport your rabbit to the Great Outdoors.

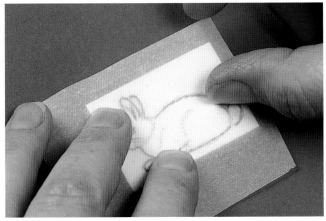

1 Draw or trace the rabbit on tracing paper (use the template on page 78 or an image of your choice). Add detail lines inside the image and transfer it to your carving block.

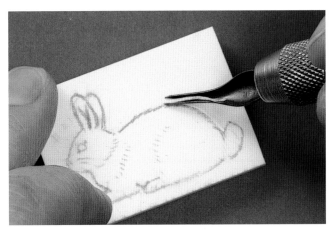

2 Carve along the outside of the penciled outline with the small V-tip gouge.

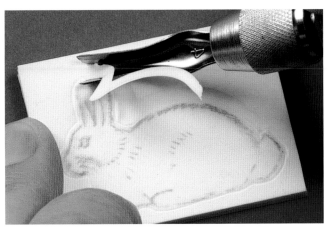

3 Carve along the guideline you carved in step 2 using your large U-tip gouge. This will give you a thicker line.

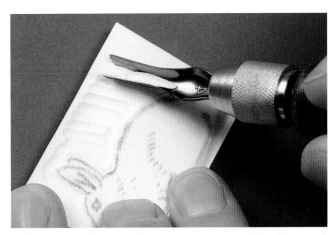

4 Use your large U-tip gouge to remove all background material outside the guideline, up to about ⅛ inch (3 mm) from the edge of the stamp.

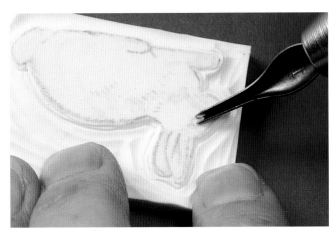

5 Using the small V-tip gouge, carefully pick out details—inside of ear, eyes, fur, etc.

6 Use the small V-tip gouge to carve small detail lines around the rabbit's legs. When finished, ink the stamp with a light-colored ink pad, and see where the image needs fine-tuning.

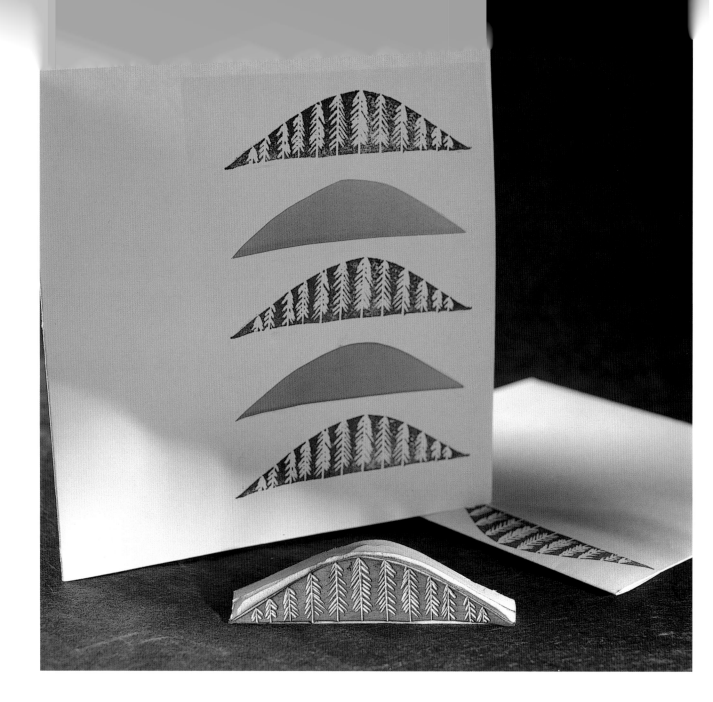

Pine Trees on a Hillside

This versatile stamp has a simple but appealing shape. Use it alone on a card or writing paper, or combine it with other landscape elements, such as the mountain and clouds on page 32, or the pine trees on page 44. You could also echo the shape of the stamp in a cutout, and back it with vellum, as shown here.

YOU WILL NEED

Carving material, roughly 2 x 3 inches (5.1 x 7.6 cm)

Pencil

Small V-tip gouge

Large U-tip gouge

Craft knife

1 Lightly pencil in a gently curved hill shape.

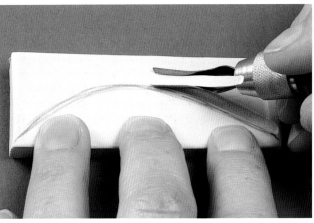

2 With the large U-tip gouge, carve on or along this guideline. Remove the background material.

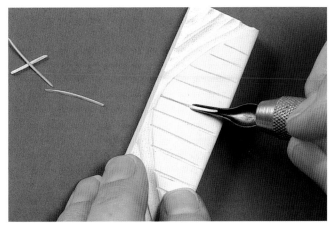

3 Lightly pencil in vertical guidelines inside the hill shape, about ¼ inch (6 mm) apart. These are the pine tree trunks.

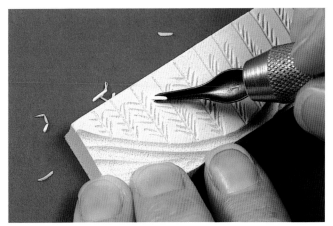

4 The tree branches can be carved freehand, or you can pencil in more guidelines. Use the small V-tip gouge to carve away from the pine tree trunks in short, regular, light strokes. For each tree, you will carve downward on either side of the trunk line you carved.

5 Use the craft knife to trim away the excess material outside the image (this allows you to place the hill stamp more accurately when stamping).

Pinwheels and Circles

Intricate designs can be composed from very simple elements. The idea for this stamp came from two different sources: a photo of a hooked rug and the view of a logging truck from the back. Pinwheels and concentric rings remind me of both images. Carve one stamp with the whole design, or carve several elements separately and combine them into any colors and shapes you need. When using the single large stamp, try using a rainbow ink pad (an ink pad with several stripes of colors), or use special marker pens to color individual circles, then print.

YOU WILL NEED

Carving material, 3⅞ x 2½ inches (9.8 x 6.4 cm)

Pencil

Tracing paper (optional)

Small V-tip gouge

Large U-tip gouge

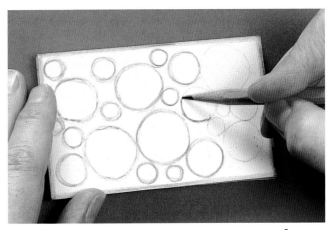

1 Draw a narrow border around the edges of the carving block. Sketch the drawing directly on the carving block. Start drawing larger circles (roughly 1 inch [2.5 cm] in diameter) in a random pattern inside the border. If you wish, use your pencil to designate which areas will be left to print dark and which areas will be carved away.

2 Draw random small circles (approximately ⅝ inch [1.6 cm] in diameter) in between the large circles. The circles can touch, but not overlap.

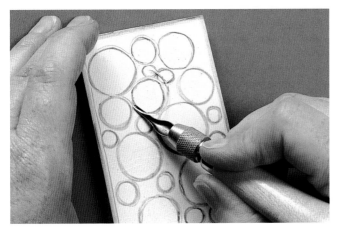

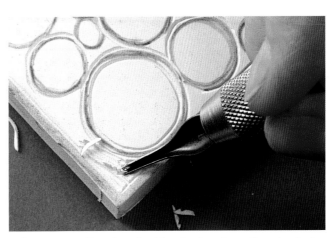

3 Carve along the guideline of each circle with the small V-tip gouge.

4 Carve a line just inside the border of each circle, leaving a rim for each one, then carve away the background material between the circles with the large U-tip gouge. If the large gouge won't fit in your small spaces, use a small gouge.

5 At random, carve some of the circles into pie slices. On some of these, carve away alternating slices. Carve the remaining circles into spirals or concentric circles.

Cut your carving material into small squares. Carve a large, medium, or small circle on each square. On some of the circles, create pie designs, and create spirals on others. Combine your stamps to make a large design, or use them individually as accent elements.

Horse

This horse image was inspired by the ancient cave paintings discovered in Lascaux, France. The simple shape and fluid lines of the horse lend themselves well to hand-carving. Overlap stamped images to create your own herd of running horses, or put several together on one block. Note that the horse's legs fade away in this design. No hooves! This is known as "artistic license."

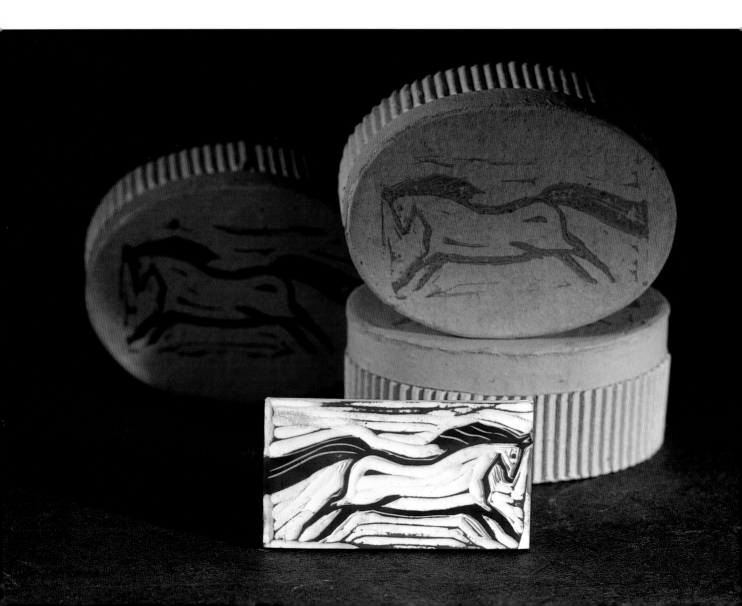

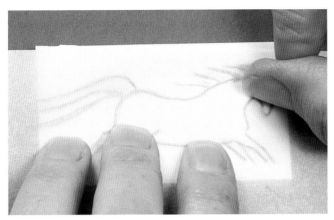

1 Draw or trace an image of a running horse onto tracing paper. Use the template on page 78 or a horse image of your choice. You can draw directly onto the carving block if you prefer, but remember that when you print your stamp, your horse will be running in the opposite direction. Transfer the image to your carving block.

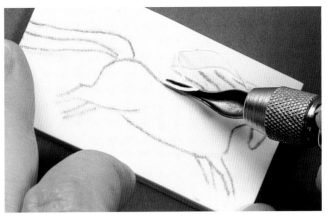

2 Carve a guideline around your penciled outline with the small V-tip gouge.

3 Remove all background material outside your guideline with the large U-tip gouge. If you want to create a border, either pencil it in before carving or leave a rough outline around the edge of the stamp.

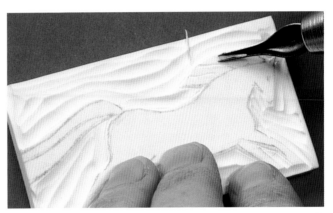

4 Add detail lines in the mane and tail with your small gouge, as shown in the photo. If you want to leave the horse's eye as a solid dot, carve around a tiny dot for the eye with the small V-tip gouge.

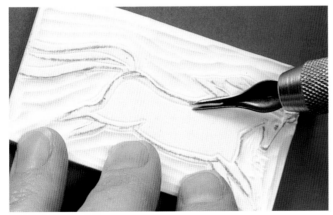

5 Carve a guideline inside your penciled outline.

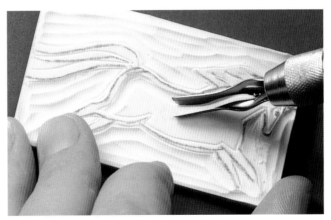

6 Use the large gouge to remove the material inside the guideline you carved in step 5. Use the small gouge to get into tight spots. You can leave the horse's lower legs and muzzle uncarved, for a more dramatic line. Ink up your image and stamp, then carve away any areas that need a little extra work.

Carving material
(one block for each letter in your word)

Samples of letters you want to carve

Pencil

Tracing paper (optional)

Small V-tip gouge

Large U-tip gouge (optional)

Ink pad in a light color

Scrap paper

Words

Learn how to carve individual letters, and you'll be able to add any word you want to your stamping projects—cards, gift tags, stationery, even three-dimensional objects, such as a mug or a plate. Once you learn to rotate your carving block, you'll be successful at getting around the curves of rounded letters. Words are great background and collage elements, or use them as a part of your design for faux postage.

1 Trace the first letter you wish to carve.

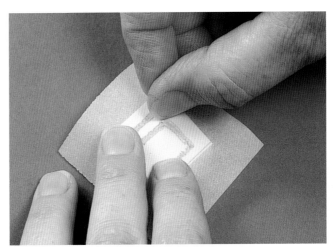

2 Lay the tracing paper penciled-side down onto the carving block. Scratch the back of the tracing paper so the tracing transfers to the carving block.

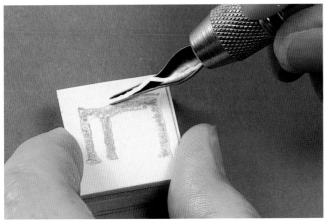

3 With the small V-tip gouge, carve a light, shallow line around the outside of the penciled line of your letter.

4 Rotate your block to get smooth carving lines and turns.

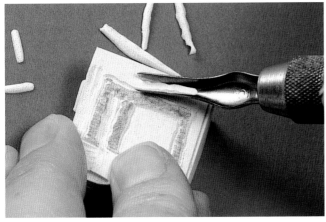

5 Remove background the material outside the letter you're carving. Ink the stamp with the light-colored ink pad, and do a test print on scrap paper. Make adjustments to your carving if needed.

6 Proceed to carve the rest of the letters in the word following steps 1 through 5.

Daffodils

You can find design inspiration just about anywhere. This daffodil was adapted from an illustrations of daffodils in a bulb catalog. The motif is perfect for spring-theme items or gifts. You can either use marking pens to color the actual carving before you stamp, or color in with pencils, markers, or chalk after you stamp.

Carving material, 4½ x 3½ inches
(11.4 x 8.9 cm)

Pencil

Daffodil template on page 78 (optional)

Tracing paper (optional)

Small V-tip gouge

Medium U-tip gouge

Ink pad in light color

Scrap paper

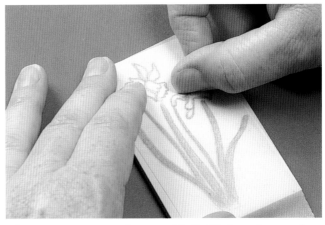

1 Draw or trace an image of daffodils (use the template on page 78 or a design of your choice), and transfer the tracing to your carving block. If you prefer, use a different transfer method (see pages 12–13).

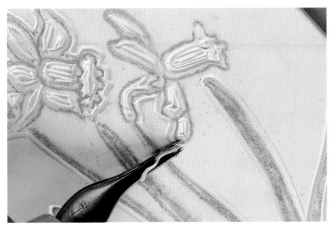

2 With the small V-tip gouge, carve guidelines inside the flowers. Remove the material inside these areas. With the same small gouge, carve a guideline along the outside of the flowers and stems.

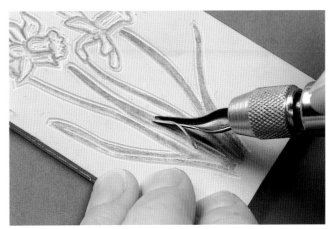

3 Carve detail lines inside the leaves.

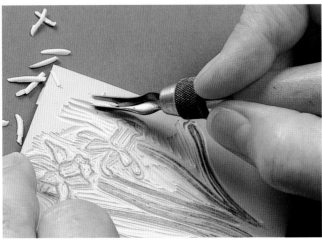

4 With the medium U-shaped gouge, carve away the background material along the outside guideline.

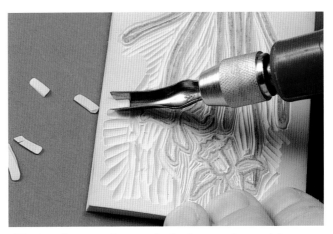

5 Continue carving out the background material, scooping up to about ⅛ inch (3 mm) from the edge of the block. This will give your border a hand-hewn look. Ink your block and test stamp the image, then make any necessary adjustments to your carving.

Oak Tree

You'll find lots of different uses for this versatile tree image. Combine it with small leaves or simple flower shapes for different seasons of the year. Add simple cloud shapes in green to create a fully leafed-out tree. Stamp your tree bare for a Halloween treatment and place a few stamped pumpkins at its base. You could even leave an uncarved oval on a branch area and stamp a small owl to perch there. The possibilities are endless!

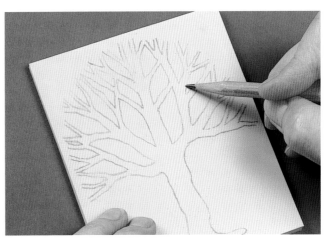

1 Trace and transfer the tree design to the carving block, or use the transfer method of your choice. Use the template on page 79 if you can't find an oak tree image you like.

2 Check to make sure that all the lines transferred. If certain areas didn't transfer, realign the template and transfer again, or use a pencil to fill in the missing areas.

TIP

You may find it difficult to print this oversized stamp. See pages 22–23 for information on how to use a printing press and other methods for stamping oversize stamps.

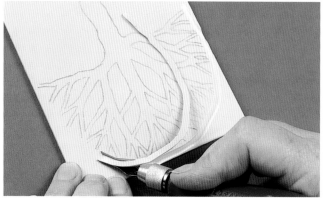

3 Carve a guideline around the outside edge of the tree branches with the large U-tip gouge. This does not need to be exact—it simply helps maintain a pleasing outline for the tree branches.

4 Still using the large gouge, carve along the outside of the guideline of the trunk and the roots.

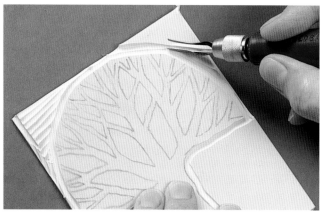

5 Remove all the background material from around the outline you just carved with the large gouge. Carve away from, not toward, the tree image.

6 Pencil in the tree design to create a silhouette (rather than a pencil outline). This will help you see where to carve—you won't carve anything that isn't penciled in.

7 Remove all the background material from between the branches. Use the large gouge in the larger areas and the small gouge in tighter areas. If you can't get the small gouge into tight corners, use a craft knife to carefully cut into these corners neatly, then use the small gouge to gently remove these little bits.

8 Carve away the background material around the trunk and roots of the tree with the large gouge. When you're finished, ink the stamp and test on a piece of scrap paper. Remove any extra material you don't want in the final image.

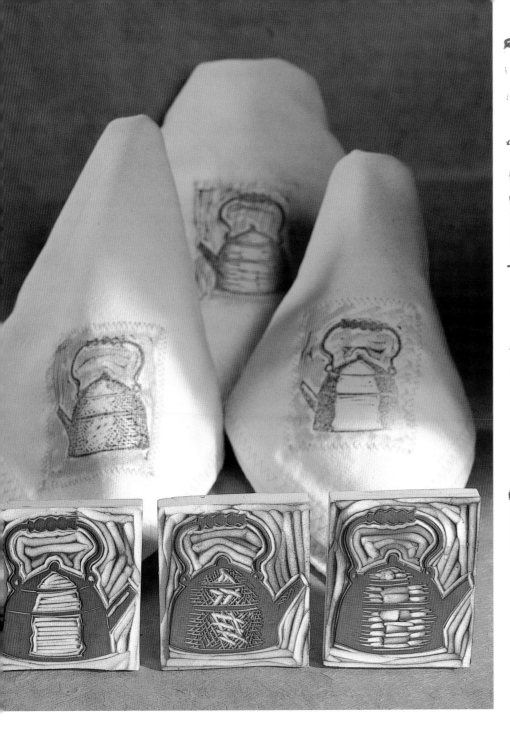

Teakettle

Creating shadows and shading can be challenging for any carver. Some carvers find them so intimidating, they bypass the technique altogether. Don't be afraid of the dark! This little teakettle image shows three different ways to depict shading. The original drawing was a simple line drawing, and you can carve the kettle that way, too.

1 Draw or trace and transfer the image to the carving block. Pencil in a guideline of where the shadow will fall, and fill it in with pencil. (I penciled in the shadows on the transfer paper).

2 Using the small V-tip gouge, carve inside the rings connecting the handle.

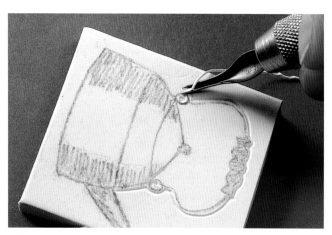

3 Carve along the outside of the kettle with the small V-tip gouge, starting with the handle.

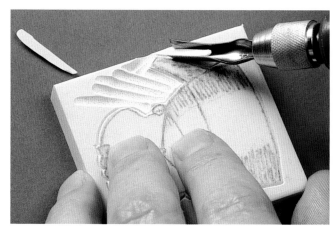

4 Remove all background material from outside the kettle with the large U-tip gouge.

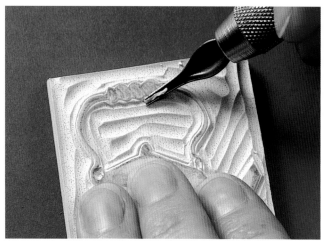

5 Carve out the background material inside the kettle handle with the small V-tip gouge.

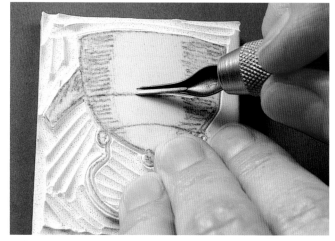

6 Carve the outlines of the two detail lines inside the kettle (the line of the lid and the line of the seam) and the outline along the bottom middle section of the kettle.

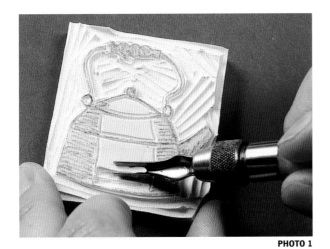

PHOTO 1

Now you have your choice of three different ways to shade. You can stop at any point and see how you like the effect.

SOLID SHADOW

Carve away the area from the top to the bottom of the kettle, in the middle of the image, being careful not to carve away the lines distinguishing the dark penciled area from the white center, as shown in photo 1. Leave the shadows as solid areas.

PHOTO 2

LINE SHADOW

Leave about ¼ inch (6 mm) of your outer shadow areas uncarved. Carve from the outside to the inside of the kettle with a small V-tip gouge. Lightly carve a column of shallow, short, widely spaced cuts right next to the solid area. As you move closer into the center of the kettle, the spacing between cuts in your columns should get closer together (see photo 2). This will progressively lighten the printed image. Finally, remove all or almost all of the carving material in the center, so it will print white, as shown in photo 3.

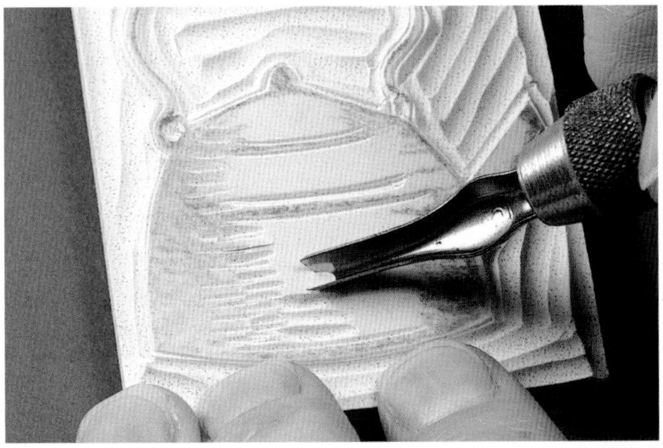

PHOTO 3

CROSS-HATCHING

Follow the instructions for line shading, but add diagonal cuts across the horizontal ones you made (see photo 4). Your lines can either get closer together or thicker as you move toward the center of the kettle.

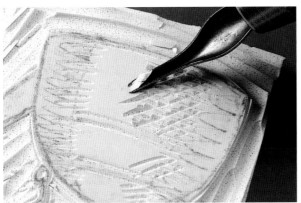

PHOTO 4

Signature

A handcarved signature stamp is a great way to individualize your corre-spondence or even your artwork. It's a little tricky to carve legible cursive letters, so start slowly. If it's easier for you, start with your first name, then carve your last name separately, and combine the two. Remember, small dings and cuts in your carving can be camouflaged in the printed version. Just fill in with a marker that's the same color as your ink pad.

Tracing paper

Pencil

Carving material
in the size of your choice

Small V-tip gouge

Large U-tip gouge (optional)

Craft knife (optional)

Ink pad in a light color

Scrap paper

1 Write your signature on the tracing paper exactly as you wish it to appear. Don't write your name directly on the carving block. It will show up backwards! For your first try at carving, you may want to write your name a little more clearly and carefully than you usually would.

2 Lay the tracing paper penciled-side down on the carving block, and scratch the back of the paper to transfer the signature to the carving block.

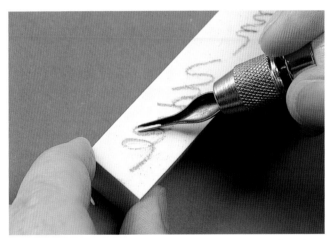

3 With the small V-tip gouge, carve a light, shallow line along the outside of the penciled line of your signature. Rotate the block to get smooth carving lines and turns.

4 When all the letters are completely traced with the small gouge, go back and carve out the loops in any a's, e's, d's, etc. TIP: If you have trouble with this method, try carving out the insides of the letters first.

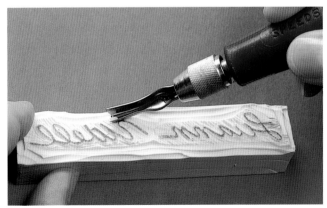

5 Remove the background material with either the large or small gouge or a craft knife. Ink the stamp with the light-colored ink pad, do a test print on scrap paper, and make adjustments to your carving.

I Love You Heart

DESIGNER: **SALLY MERICLE**

This delicate heart stamp says "I Love You" in French, the language of love! Use it to create Valentine's Day greetings cards or a gift tag for a special gift. This stamp makes a great collage element, too. You can add ribbon around the edges, or use it with embossing powder. Try stamping on a colored piece of paper and using a contrasting color ink.

1 Trace a heart image (use the template on page 79 or an image of your choice), and transfer it to your carving block. Instead of using your fingernail, try using a tool, such as the handle of a spoon, to burnish the image onto the block.

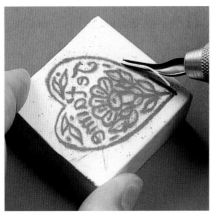

2 Carve along the outer guideline of the heart with the medium V-tip gouge.

3 Use a large U-tip gouge to carve away the background material outside the outer guideline.

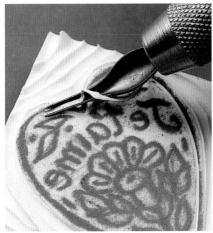

4 Carve along the inside of your guideline with the small V-tip gouge.

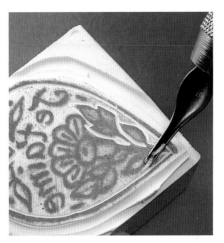

5 Carve outside the guidelines of the leaves and flowers, then carve inside the guidelines.

6 Create carving guidelines above and below the phrase and carve inside the a, e's, and m.

7 Carve away the material between the letters.

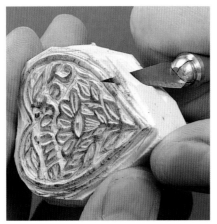

8 Use a craft knife to trim down the material outside the heart guideline, creating a heart-shaped stamp.

Crow

There is a group of crows that hangs out in the tall pine trees outside my studio. Their bold nature and heartily raucous calls amuse me. Their inky, dark silhouettes work well as simple, solid images for carving. Add a hand-hewn looking border, and you have a very effective design. You can transform this image into a faux postage stamp by stamping the word "crow" in tiny letters inside the border afterwards.

1 Trace and transfer the crow image (use the template on page 79 or the image of your choice). You can also draw the crow directly onto your carving block, leaving a bit of space at the edge of the block for the carved border.

YOU WILL NEED

Carving material, 2½ x 2½ inches (6.4 x 6.4 cm)

Tracing paper

Crow template on page 79 (optional)

Pencil

Small V-tip gouge

Medium or large U-tip gouge

Ink pad in light color

Scrap paper

Alphabet stamps (optional)

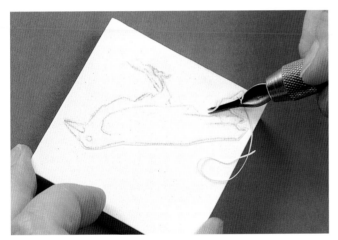

2 With the small V-tip gouge, carve a guideline along the outside of the penciled line.

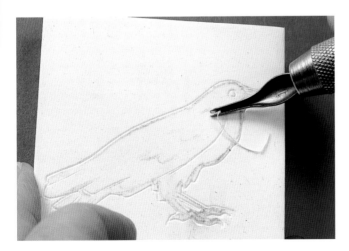

3 Add fine detail lines, indicating the line of the wing and the hairy feathers around the bill, legs, etc. Carve a tiny circle for the eye.

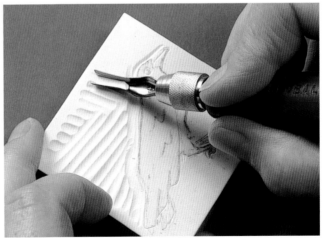

4 With the medium or large U-tip gouge, carve a wide outline around the crow, using the fine carved outline as a guide. Carve wide strokes away from the crow image, scooping up to just inside the block's edge, about ⅟₁₆ to ⅛ inch (1.6 to 3 mm). You can radiate all these strokes from the crow, or carve them perpendicular to each edge. Ink the image with light-colored ink and stamp a test image. Adjust your carving if necessary. Add the word "crow" with letter stamps, if you like.

Dragonfly

The charming and elegant dragonfly is a popular motif that you can add to almost any project. Check insect guides for images to trace and carve. Don't be intimidated by the sophisticated look of the wings—there are several ways to handle the design. You can start with a simple solid wing and advance to more detailed treatments as you improve your carving skills. Just follow your guidelines as usual, and you'll be impressed with the results you achieve.

Carving block,
3 x 3½ inches (7.6 x 8.9 cm)

Pencil

Dragonfly template on page 79 (optional)

Tracing paper
(or transfer method of your choice)

Small V-tip gouge

Large U-tip gouge

Craft knife (optional)

Ink pad in light color

Scrap paper

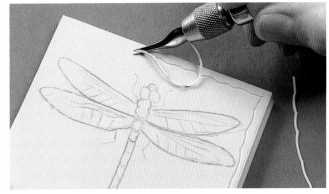

1 Trace and transfer a dragonfly image (use the template on page 79 or an image of your choice), or draw one directly onto your block. If you want to simplify the design, leave out the detail inside the wings. Use the small V-tip gouge to carve a free-form wriggly border all the way around the stamp, about ⅛ inch (3 mm) from the edge.

2 Carve along the outside pencil line of your dragonfly with the small V-tip gouge to create a guideline.

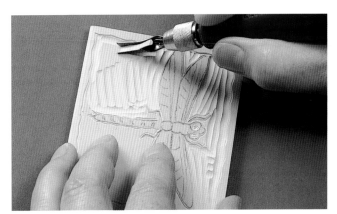

3 Carve away the background material with the large U-tip gouge. Use the small V-tip gouge or the craft knife to get into tight areas.

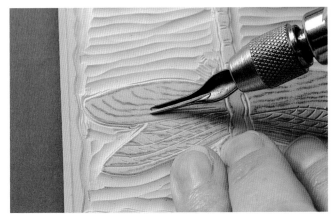

4 Make tiny detail lines on the body and tail of the dragonfly, and carve the delicate tracery of the wings. Carve small circles or ovals for the eyes, being careful to leave a thin outline.

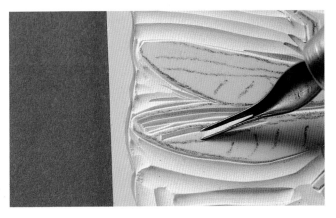

VARIATION

An alternative is to carve out the inside area of the wings, leaving them outlined. You can then leave them open or fill in details with a marker, or add simple tracery details in the wings and carve around them.

Par Avion Postage Stamp

Add wings to your air mail! You can create this stamp as a single image, but it's easier to carve and more versatile to use when you carve the words and wings separately. Use any size block to create any size postage stamp border you want. Add postal words such as "par avion" or "faux poste." Wings are delightful flights of fancy to use with any number of different images: heavenly dogs, winged horses, flying fish...Use your imagination!

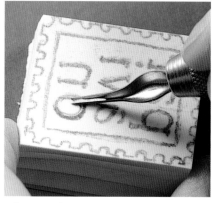

1 Use the postage stamp template on page 79 to make a stamp border or draw your own. Transfer the border to your carving block. Trace the letters for par avion and transfer them to the block, inside the inner guidelines. Carve the insides of the closed letters—p, a, and o—with a small V-tip gouge before carving the outline of the letters.

YOU WILL NEED

1 carving block,
1½ x 2 inches (3.8 x 5.1 cm)

2 carving blocks,
1½ x 1 inch (3.8 cm x 2.5 cm) each

Postage stamp template, page 79

Pencil

Tracing paper

Small V-tip gouge

Medium U-tip gouge

2 Carve along the outside of the letters with the small V-tip gouge. TIP: If you should err in the carving of the "par avion" letters, carve out all the material inside the inner guidelines. You can carve the phrase on a separate block of carving material, and stamp it inside the stamp border later.

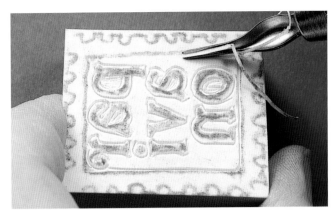

3 Carve along the inside guideline of the stamp border, then carve away the background material inside the inner guideline.

4 For the perforations, hold the medium U-tip gouge almost straight up and down, and line it up with the scallops that suggest perforations. Push down firmly—this will scoop out small rounded chunks from the edge of the carving block. Continue to scoop, following the guidelines around the perimeter of the stamp.

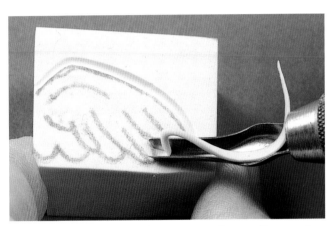

5 Trace and transfer the wings to the smaller carving blocks. Carve the outline of each wing stamp with a large or small gouge.

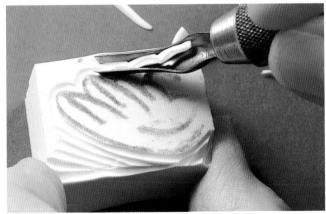

6 Remove the background material from outside the wing guideline.

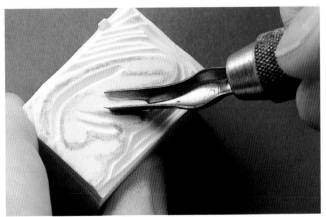

7 Carve around the detail lines inside the wing stamp, taking care to leave all the material that is penciled.

GALLERY

ABOVE LEFT: **NICKIE ROMANUCK**, *Clowning Around*; carved rubber, design from Masquerade & Carnival, Butterick Pattern Company, 1897.

ABOVE RIGHT: **MAGDA LAGERWERF**, *Tulip*, 1999; custom carving block, four-color printing, oil-based ink.

BELOW LEFT: **STACIA SCHWARTZ**, *Cave Art Box*, 2001; Handcarved stamps on paper, folded into a unit origami box and lid.

BELOW RIGHT: **JANICE BRYANT**, *English Cottage*, 2001; custom carving block (three stamps), ink, colored pencil, pencil.

ABOVE LEFT: **ERIKA RADICH**, *Figure 1* (LEFT), *Figure 3* (CENTER), 2001; carved rubber stamps.

ABOVE RIGHT AND RIGHT CENTER: **MAGDA LAGERWERF**, *Trade Cards*; eraser carvings.

LEFT: **MARY BARTOP**, *Round Trip*, 2001; accordion book stamped with carved erasers.

BELOW LEFT: **SUSAN MCBRIDE**, *Untitled*, 2001; handcarved stamp on paper painted with watercolors.

BELOW RIGHT: **LYNN D. TROLDAHL HERSHBERGER**, *Self Portrait*, 2000–2001; carved block.

TOP: **JANE ARNAL**, *The Land Lady's Patio/Garden*, 2000; custom carving block, water-based ink, watercolor paints.

CENTER LEFT: **LUANN UDELL**, *The Lascaux Stag*, 2001; handcarved stamps on paper.

CENTER RIGHT: **JULIE HAGAN BLOCH**, *Magic Rocks 2*, 2000; custom carving block.

BELOW: **ANGEL WAHBY**, *Cleansing*, 2001; eraser carving stamped on handmade paper, melted onto handmade soap with wax.

BELOW RIGHT: **SUE NAN DOUGLASS**, *I Saw the Angel...* (*RUBBERSTAMPMADENESS Magazine*, Nov./Dec. 1994); custom carving block, ink, brush markers, colored pencils.

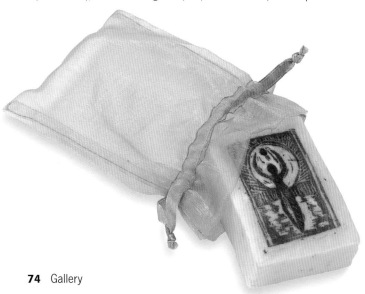

ABOVE LEFT: **SHARON SCHEEL**, *Hitchin' a Ride*, 2001; custom carving block, pigment ink.

ABOVE RIGHT: **ANDREA TAYLOR**, *Clock*, 2001; custom carving block, cotton swabs and dye-based ink pad for background.

LEFT: **KIM CUNNIGHAM**, *The Gibbon*, 1997; linoleum tools on carving material, printed with oil-based blockprint ink and hand-colored with watercolors.

BELOW: **MAGDA LAGERWERF**, *Moi*, 1998; eraser carving.

LEFT: **CATHERINE SIMPSON**, *Circle Squared #3*, 2001; vinyl eraser carving, permanent inks.

BOTTOM LEFT: **BARBARA ZARETSKY**, *Scarf*, 2000; 100% silk, carved rubber blocks; borders brush painted; center roller painted; textile paint.

BOTTOM RIGHT: **LINDA MILLIGAN**, *Jewel Beetle II*, 2001; custom carving block, dye-based inks, embossing ink.

BELOW: **MARCIA L. BALONIS**, *Sassy Lady*, 2001; custom carving block

Jewel Beetle II   3/14/2001

ABOVE LEFT: **KINGA BRITSCHGI**, *Architectural Series II*, 2000; carved block, water soluble printing ink.

ABOVE RIGHT: **SUSANNA LAKNER**, *Woman Art*, 1999–2001; stamp sheet, rubber stamps.

LEFT: **VICTORIA BOLTON**, *Carving Consortium Artist's Café*, 2001; carved rubber, pigment inks, embossing powder, gel pen.

BELOW: **SHEILA CUNNINGHAM**, *One of Those Days*, 1999; handcarved, center image stamped on wet acetate, stamped faces copied onto transparency film, polymer clay cover from mold of stamped face.

TEMPLATES

Chick and Egg, *page 40*

Globe Stamp, *page 30*

Rabbit, *page 44*

Horse, *page 50*

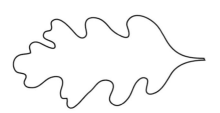

Oak Leaves, *page 34*

5

pesce postale

Fish Post, *page 37*

Daffodils, *page 54*